D1069765

Cover: Photograph of a painting by Tompkins Harrison
Matteson (1813–1884), entitled *The Dedication of the
Dudley Observatory at Albany, August 28, 1856*

2 Prof. Joseph Henry, Secretary,
   Smithsonian Institution
3 Prof. Benjamin Silliman, Yale
   University
4 Dr. Thomas Hun, Albany
5 Rev. D. Eben Halley, Albany
6 President Edward Hitchcock,
   Amherst
7 William B. Rogers, State
   Geologist, Pennsylvania
9 Henry R. Schoolcraft,
   Washington
10 Mrs. Blandina Dudley, Albany
11 Thomas Olcott, Albany
12 Chancellor Gerrit Y. Lansing,
   Albany
13 Gideon Hawley, Regent at
   Large, Smithsonian Institution
14 Ezra P. Prentice, Albany
15 Rev. Dr. William B. Sprague,
   Albany
20 Sir William Logan, Montreal
21 Orlando Meads, Albany
22 Dr. Philip Ten Eyck, Albany
23 Alexander D. Bache, Sup't. U.S.
   Coast Survey
24 Prof. Benjamin A. Gould,
   Director, Dudley Observatory
25 Hon. Horatio Seymour,
   Ex-Governor of New York
26 General Peter Gansevoort,
   Albany

27 Hon. John V. L. Pruyn, Albany
28 Martin B. Anderson, President,
   University of Rochester
29 Prof. Benjamin Peirce,
   Harvard College
1 Hon. Edward Everett,
   U.S. Senator
30 Dr. James MacNaughton,
   Albany
31 Governor Myron H. Clark
32 Ex-Gov. Washington Hunt
33 Dr. Alfred L. Loomis, New York
34 Victor M. Rice, Sup't. Public
   Instruction
35 Prof. Louis Agassiz, Cambridge
36 Dr. Ebenezer Emmons, Albany
37 Prof. James D. Dana,
   New Haven
38 Prof. James Hall, Albany
39 W. C. Redfield, 1st President,
   A.A.A.S.
40 Prof. Samuel H. Hammond
41 Prof. Charles Davies,
   U.S. Military Academy
42 B. P. Johnson, President,
   State Agricultural Society
43 Prof. Dr. James H. Armsby,
   Albany
44 Hon. Ira Harris, Albany
45 Hon. Amasa J. Parker, Albany
46 Amos Dean, L.L.D., Albany
47 Hon. Robert H. Pruyn, Albany

The picture represents the service in the Albany Academy Park at the time of the dedication of the Dudley Observatory, August 28, 1856. Hon. Edward Everett is seen delivering the oration in the presence of the American Association for the Advancement of Science and a large body of other distinguished men. . . .

The lady in a bonnet at the lower left is Mrs. Dudley, the donor of the observatory. She is dressed in gray and seated in a mahogany chair upholstered in dark red. Red, white, and blue bunting on the stand at the left. Striped red, white, and blue tent. American flags are draped in upper right corner. Professor Louis Agassiz, the man at the right holding a straw hat on his knee, wears a black coat, white shirt, stock, collar, and tie and a pearl gray waistcoat and pearl gray trousers. The man below him, who is writing on the edge of the platform, wears a pearl gray coat and waistcoat, a white shirt and collar, and a black stock. He has brown hair and a brown beard. Brownish carpet with dull red figures, on platform. Some of the ladies at lower left and right wear red shawls or cloaks. The table is covered with a dull green cloth with a red stripe near the edge. A large gray building can be seen through the opening in the tent at upper left.

Photograph of the painting: *Courtesy of The Albany Institute of History and Art.* Description of the painting: *Courtesy of the National Portrait Gallery, Smithsonian Institution.* Key to the painting: *Courtesy of The Frick Art Reference Library.*

Nature and
the American Mind

Louis Agassiz, ca. 1863

*"Since Benjamin Franklin, we had never had among
us a person of more popularly impressive type."*
—WILLIAM JAMES, 1896

EDWARD LURIE

NATURE AND
THE AMERICAN MIND:
Louis Agassiz
and the Culture of
Science

SCIENCE HISTORY PUBLICATIONS

NEW YORK

First published in the United States by
Science History Publications
a division of
Neale Watson Academic Publications, Inc.
156 Fifth Avenue, New York 10010

© 1974 by Science History Publications

(CIP Data on final page)

ISBN 0-88202-011-0

Designed and manufactured
in the U.S.A.

500.9
L97

QH
31
.A2
L83
1974

Dedicated to the memory of

Alfred S. Romer

Contents

Nature and

the American Mind

HISTORIANS are true to their craft if they attempt to separate reality from myth, event from romance, and fact from historiographic fancy. The historian, while heeding Eva Reichmann's injunction to "pierce through the tangle of present-day happenings towards an understanding of his place in the maze,"[1] must perform another equally difficult task: He must untangle the web in which the past has consciously cocooned itself against the valid perceptions of it by contemporary students. This dual responsibility can force the historian into contemporary web-spinning, causing further difficulty for future historians. Josiah Royce understood this problem when, in assessing the value of Hegel's philosophy, he observed, "almost everybody has forgotten what it means and has therefore come to accept it as true."[2] Henry Adams, whose famed autobiography, *The Education of Henry Adams,* must be regarded as the epitome of web-spinning, concealing both the acts and the motives of the actors from future historians, gave some hint of this

dilemma when, from the vantage point of 1906, he
wrote of his life that

> only with that understanding—as a consciously as-
> senting member in full partnership with . . . society
> —had his education an interest to himself or to
> others. As it happened, he never got to the point of
> playing the game at all; he lost himself in the study
> of it, watching the errors of the players; but this is
> the only interest in the story, which otherwise has no
> moral and little incident.[3]

As Ernest Samuels and James K. Flack have shown in
their penetrating analyses of the influence of Adams
and others of his elitist friends, such pleading in fact
revealed deep involvement in nineteenth-century culture and ideas, hidden for reasons that now comprise
the historian's burden.[4] That burden is given a fine
edge by the words of the late W. H. Auden, who in *The
Double Man,* provided an insight into the problem of
untangling the web of the past, interwoven with attitudes toward the dead and the living:

> The situation of our time
> Surrounds us like a baffling crime
> There lies the body half-undressed
> We all had reason to detest
> And all are suspects and involved
> Until the mystery is solved

> And under lock and key the cause
> That makes a nonsense of our laws.*[5]*

The difficulty of laying bare the true physiognomy of the past and undoing the baffling crime is compounded by the constraints and the attitudes of the historian's own time. It is the more difficult when the historian is confronted with the tangle behind the tangle that exists when he deals with a man who was himself a body half-undressed by his own age.

This situation, then, and our efforts to untangle the web are strikingly illustrated by the degree to which we approach an understanding of the life in America of Jean Louis Rodolphe Agassiz.

In the early months of 1874, Agassiz's New England contemporary, James Russell Lowell, was in Italy, whose southern warmth had often cheered New Englanders such as Henry Adams and Henry James. The southern air, however, did not long provide that sanctuary for Lowell; as he described his mental state in that exemplar of New England elite literary fashion, the *Atlantic Monthly*:

> . . . with vague, mechanic eyes,
> I scanned the festering news we half despise . . .
> When suddenly,
> As happens if the brain, from overweight
> Of blood, infect the eye,

Three tiny words grew lurid as I read,
And reeled commingling: *Agassiz is dead!*

The profound sense of loss was felt by Brahmin and
commoner alike and is with us still. On December 14,
1873, Agassiz succumbed to the physical and mental
exhaustion that had marked the last decade of his life
in the United States. Lowell's grief revealed the sense
of gratitude and awe that Agassiz had inspired:

We have not lost him all; he is not gone . . .
The beauty of his better self lives on
In minds he touched with fire, in many an eye . . .
He was a Teacher . . .
Whose living word still stimulates the air . . .

The biographer must seek to recapture that enthusiasm
for science and culture inspired by Agassiz's better self.
But the character of our own time makes the mystery
harder to solve, since mere adulation leaves the body
still only half-undressed. Lowell understood this problem, ending his epitaph with the words:

In endless file shall loving scholars come
The glow of his transmitted touch to share,
And trace his features with an eye less dim
Than ours whose sense familiar wont makes numb.[6]

The less dim eye of the historian must not be clouded
by the omniscience of that beauty both rightly and

mythically attributed to Agassiz, nor made less perceptive by the romance kindled by files of loving scholars whose later efforts only deepened the mystery. A culture hero such as Agassiz achieves status to the degree that his public acts remain shrouded in what George F. Hoar termed, in describing Ralph Waldo Emerson, "a mystery calm and intense."

Considering Agassiz's significance for America I may, I suspect, have spent too long at this effort, so that my assessments may represent the same kind of web-spinning I have cautioned against. I am strongly tempted to take refuge behind the words of Rosalind Russell in the musical comedy *Wonderful Town,* who, when asked to give a summary of the plot of *Moby Dick,* said, "Well, it's about this whale."

But the responsibility of subjective judgment forces the historian to analyze the meaning of the color of the whale, and the motives of both the animal and his pursuers. This commitment attracted still another poet and cultural critic, Ezra Pound, to the syncretism of romance and science that epitomized Agassiz. Writing of the vapidity of American culture in the mid-nineteenth century, Pound ascribed this condition as due

to its being offered as "something like" English culture, but rather less lively; something to join Tennyson in "The Abbey" perhaps, but nothing quite as exciting as Browning or Fitzgerald's *Rubiyat.*

To Pound, America could boast of only a few rare heroic men, and one of these was Agassiz because, "apart from his brilliant achievements in natural science," he "ranks as a writer of prose, precise knowledge of his subject leading to exactitude of expression."[7] Lowell, who described American intellect and culture at this time as "level in monotone," would doubtless have applauded Pound's estimate of Agassiz, whose life distinguished him from the common run of American taste-makers and style-shapers.

No matter what his particular American endeavor, Agassiz consistently undertook it with optimism, boundless zeal, enthusiasm, and a faith that the potential of American genius needed to be encouraged to greater heights of achievement. In an age of mediocrity in politics, the absence of a common national purpose about the future of man and society, a prevalent lack of distinction in common and higher education, little public value placed on creative work in science or literature, and a dearth of men with the drive to ameliorate these conditions, Agassiz was almost unique both as a man and as a symbol of purpose. Metaphorically, he might be seen as an Emerson who joined thought and action, an Adams who enjoyed playing the game for the high stakes that winning it would bring, or a Whitman who could employ science to gain the affection, sympathy, and support of various publics. Agassiz was keenly aware of the potentialities inherent in the national character, and his determination to exploit them won him friends and foes, laurels and blame; but his accomplishments were at once real and spiritual and these left the nation richer for his presence.

No other man in mid-nineteenth century America could have established its first great research museum, served as the catalyst behind the organization of its leading institutions of science—the American Association for the Advancement of Science, the National Academy of Sciences, and the Smithsonian Institution —combined with others to turn Harvard from an old-time college into a modern University, gained more monies for science than any other contemporary, and educated the most distinguished aggregation of students of natural history that one American scientist ever had trained.

Agassiz's cultural value lies, therefore, in his achieving for the writing, teaching, and popular appreciation of natural science what other rare men of his time accomplished in other realms—men such as Raphael Pumpelly, Clarence King, and John Wesley Powell in the study of geology and the cultural appreciation of science. The same was true of Henry Adams in the writing of history. His role of cultural gadfly is ably demonstrated in his novel *Democracy.[8]* In his outstanding leadership, Theodore Roosevelt, who captured the popular imagination with his vision of the heroic servant of the people whose love of nature would advance culture and help to recapture it from the depredations wrought equally by neo-Jacksonian expansionists and robber-baron exploiters, was of very similar significance.*[9]*

It should not be surprising that Agassiz's life found strong admirers in men such as Henry Adams and Theodore Roosevelt, since they saw in Agassiz the qualities they found lacking in America. Those attributes comprised a sense of purpose, a belief in the potentiality inherent in the future, and a faith in education and knowledge that, comparable to the belief system of the founding fathers, would advance national culture so that the United States need not be viewed as culturally underdeveloped by the civilized nations of Europe.

That cultural deficiency was best described by a student of nineteenth-century culture, George Santayana, who, because of birth, religion, and the circumstance of career, was both within and outside the often imitative, uninspiring life of the American mind as directed from Boston and the Harvard Yard. Thus did Santayana depict the American scene about one hundred years ago:

About the middle of the nineteenth century, in the quiet sunshine of provincial prosperity, New England had an Indian summer of the mind; and an agreeable reflective literature showed how brilliant

that russet and yellow season could be. There were
poets, historians, orators, preachers, most of whom
had studied foreign literatures and had travelled;
they demurely kept up with the times . . . But it was
all a harvest of leaves; these worthies had an expur-
gated and barren conception of life; theirs was the
purity of sweet old age. Sometimes they made at-
tempts to rejuvenate their minds by broaching native subjects . . . but the inspiration did not seem
much more American than that of Swift or . . . Châ-
teaubriand. These cultivated writers lacked native
roots and fresh sap because the American intellect
itself lacked them. Their culture was half a pious
survival, half an intentional acquirement; it was not
the inevitable flowering of a fresh experience . . . If
any one, like Walt Whitman, penetrated to the feelings and images which the American scene was able
to breed out of itself, and filled them with a frank
and broad afflatus of his own . . . he misrepresented
the conscious minds of cultivated Americans; in
them the head as yet did not belong to the trunk.[*10*]

Henry Adams understood the temper of the mind in
New England and, by extension, in the United States
when he identified his sensibility as unsuited for it. Re-
flecting on the life he was determined to lead amidst
the materialist gainers and seekers of a world that had
disavowed rationalism, republican virtue, and the val-

ues of order, he saw himself as futile. In words that actually masked the power he held to make culture heroic, Adams said of himself:

> Had he been born in Jerusalem under the shadow
> of the Temple . . . under the name of Israel Cohen,
> he would scarcely have been more distinctly branded,
> and not much more heavily handicapped in the races
> of the coming century . . . [*11*]

To escape the effects of cultural vapidity and narrow materialism, the mid-nineteenth century required rare men at once able to play its game, but under rules of their *own* making; men who were not always agreeable; who acted more than they reflected; who were ahead of their times rather than comfortably attuned to them; who could awaken the nation to the possibilities of the flowering of fresh experience. Such a man was Louis Agassiz. By artfully dominating and defining the subject of nature, he could bend the rules of the game to satisfy the larger good, and he could tie together the head and the heart.

Theodore Lyman, another Brahmin, understood these qualities in Lowell's beloved Teacher of Nature, when, in 1872, he wrote to Agassiz's son, Alexander, about his father's singular role in American science and life:

> Your papa . . . is a great genius . . . as to money and
> plans—he is a very great genius. When you come to

consider . . . that he is a remarkable naturalist . . .
that he has unusual power as a teacher . . . that he
is an organizer . . . that he is a man of most unusual
social power, capable of going into refined society,
and fascinating people right and left. When . . . you
consider these . . . points, you will see that there [is]
not a single man in Europe today who could do *all*
that he has done. You might find his equal as a naturalist; but then you would also find that he wore a
dirty shirt, swallowed his knife, and could only talk
German. You might find his equal in social force,
but then it would be a man who didn't know the
difference between an earth worm and a sparrow . . .
Papa has done more to excite and push forward
Natural History in the U.S. than any man who was
ever there . . . When you think of this, you will see
that it is not in reason to hope for a *Successor* to such
a steam engine.*[12]*

If Lyman's assessment is to be accepted, how is the
biographer to reconcile it with the knowledge of what
Agassiz, "his wise forefinger raised in smiling blame,"
to seize Lowell's metaphor, left undone, half-done, or
poorly fashioned? The fiery zeal that inspired him, as
it did Whitman, to plead with Americans to experience
nature directly, made him a hero of his age; but his
mania for domination at times made personal and intellectual associations equally emotional and unstable.

A young student in Agassiz's museum at Harvard,

Edward S. Morse, confided to his diary after an argument with Agassiz during which the young man—later
to become one of the world's leading marine biologists
—announced his intention of leaving the museum:

> Prof came to me . . . and was astonished and indig-
> nant that I was going to leave on such short notice.
> He showed himself in his true light . . . as long as one
> will toady to him and be content to live on nothing
> . . . so long will everything go smooth; but when one
> asserts his independence then is the man vexed and
> indignant.[*13*]

How then view the mystery of the whale with eye
less dim when neither his contemporaries nor his students agree about his true physiognomy? Henry Adams,
for example, was a student at Harvard College at the
period of Morse's complaints, and what unique appeal
of his professor led him to assert in the *Education* that:

> The only teaching that appealed to his imagination
> was a course of lectures by Louis Agassiz on the Gla-
> cial Period and Paleontology, which had more influ-
> ence on his curiosity than the rest of the college
> instruction altogether.[*14*]

That instruction was the responsibility of such nota-
bles as Lowell, Charles Eliot Norton, and others, ad-
mired by their time but fitting into the mold that
Santayana considered the harvest of leaves comprising
nineteenth-century American passivity.

Agassiz, then, was a man whose depths the historian-biographer must plumb to understand the spirit that fascinated men as diverse in time and place as Lowell, Ralph Waldo Emerson, Henry David Thoreau, John Greenleaf Whittier, Charles Darwin, James A. Garfield, and Theodore Roosevelt. Fellow scientists, notably Asa Gray and William Barton Rogers, who were affronted by Agassiz's popular appeal and alleged intellectual incompetence, could not help but secretly admire the steam engine. Even those who suffered from the results of the engineer's urge to awake Americans to do the best that was in them for the study of nature were, in the last analysis, the better for such association.

It was Pound again, many decades later, who gave voice to this twin-edged sense of value and imperiousness when he stated that "no man is equipped for modern thinking until he has understood the anecdote of Agassiz and the fish."[15] This probably apocryphal tale, of Samuel H. Scudder's experience while studying ichthyology with Agassiz at the Harvard Museum of Comparative Zoology, typifies the cultural notion that was synonymous with Agassiz's appeal—the virtue inherent in the study of "nature not books." Scudder allegedly learned this after having spent weeks dissecting a fish with no books to guide him, and succeeded to Agassiz's satisfaction only when his method had been grounded on direct observation and independent description.

Pound further compounded the untangling of the

web by attributing the mystique of personal contact
with the object itself to the comparative method of
natural science which, to him, was analogous with the
comparative method in studying aesthetics. That model
was, seemingly, what so fitted Agassiz to foster the development and advance of nineteenth-century American culture, and made his career at once virtuous,
heroic, and far in advance of the dull, routinized study
that marked most education. Agassiz's heroic character,
in the view of men separated from him by many decades, rested in its modernity, and its ability to cut
through to the heart of the matter by making every-
one—scientist, artisan, and cultivated layman—equal
under the beneficent rays of direct experience with
nature.

The nature of the whale may become more understandable if attention is centered on the one event that
encapsulated all these dedications to America. That
was the establishment, on July 8, 1873, of the Anderson
School of Natural History on Penikese Island, in the
Buzzard's Bay group of the Elizabeth Islands close by
Nantucket, Martha's Vineyard, and Woods Hole. Any
celebration of Agassiz's American Centennial must
celebrate the significance of Penikese, for it is only
through understanding the meaning and outcome of
this endeavor can the true physiognomy of the body
still half-undressed be understood.

Agassiz had always been fascinated by the study of
marine animals, and especially so after his arrival on

American shores in October of 1846. He had been similarly dedicated to advanced and popular scientific education in nature study. Public lecturing had usually included lessons of God's magnificence drawn from the radiata, the echinoderms, and the brachiopods, marine creatures whose nature provided much of the text and illustrations of his four-volume *Contributions to Natural History of the United States.[16]* In 1865, wealthy Americans and the United States Coast Survey provided the pied piper of nature study with still another opportunity to observe marine life, in the trip he took with his wife Elizabeth, a band of dedicated students (including William James), and a group of scientific assistants to study the flora and fauna of the Amazon River and its valley.[17] In 1867, and again in 1871–72, the history of marine biology once more found Agassiz, with his band of dedicated helpers, involved in surveys of the Florida reefs, as well as in a typically grand journey around South America aboard the Coast Survey steamship *Hassler,* during which he hoped, among other things, to make up his mind conclusively on the truth or falsity of Darwin's doctrine. That the scientific purposes of the *Hassler* journey remained unfulfilled was the result of failing health and poor marine technology.

Agassiz returned to Cambridge late in 1872 to find a plan for a summer school of study in natural history set in motion by his students. He immediately assumed command of it, and another foray in the cause of nature study was launched. The outcome was the gift of Penikese Island by New York tobacco merchant John Anderson, a gift that included $50,000.00 and buildings for the establishment of the school that was to bear his name. As in every Agassiz endeavor, all else was shunted aside, and, somewhat in the manner of Roosevelt storming San Juan Hill, a massive nature-study campaign was launched, gaining the aid of students, prospective teachers of science, naturalists, common workmen, and institutions to aid a cause at once divine and scientific. The establishment of the Penikese school would have gained the admiration of a Santayana or a Pound, because it was an individual, heroic effort to force Americans to confront nature first hand. Penikese was a natural culmination of the drive to educate Americans to the meaning of organic creation.

On July 8, 1873, when Agassiz told the assembled band of teachers and students that they were on the island to study nature and not learn from textbooks, he was at once exemplifying and contradicting the twin aspects of his career in Europe and the United States. Agassiz knew, by virtue of careful work done in ichthyology, marine biology, paleontology, and zoology that knowledge of nature is at once experimental, comparative, and historical. His personal library, now permanently housed at Harvard's Museum of Comparative Zoology, bears testimony to his minute and precise knowledge of facts; many of the volumes contain the owner's marginal commentaries, revealing his deep knowledge of the bibliography of nineteenth-century natural history. How then explain this seeming duality?

Agassiz's inevitable involvement in the "bookish" side of research was in contrast to the developing egalitarianism of his American years. This period saw him embrace a social democracy that witnessed his fierce defense of the Union cause, his criticism of European elitism, and a freely democratic friendship with fish vendors, lighthousekeepers, fishermen, and the armies of common folk who swarmed to his public lectures from East coast to West. This democratic vista was further attested by Agassiz's continual emphasis upon the virtue of knowing nature, the need to impart it to those who would make new discoveries, and also its familiarization to such women as Emma Graves Cary. Miss Cary, sister of "Lizzie" Agassiz, wrote to her sister Sarah of the Penikese experience that she enjoyed in the summer of 1873:

> Lizzie is very pleasant telling about the island life. [It is] . . . as if they were on a perpetual artistic picnic . . . enthusiasm, romance, open air, discomforts, very good food, science, colonies of gulls, hard work and amusement, all mixed together. The servants hurry to finish their work to come and hear the lectures, but they work well and quietly, separated from the lecture part of the big barn by the diagram board, which shuts off the pantry from the audience. Agassiz has given [his] . . . finest lectures on glaciers that

Lizzie ever heard from him. [Burt] Wilder is an admirable teacher and speaks without notes. Hawkins, the wonderful draughtsman, draws fishes on the blackboard developing them by degrees from the tail upwards till the spectators are wild with excitement. Then the . . . tired, faded teachers are sent out to learn from nature and put into practice methods of study given by Agassiz. . . . They come home to a nice dinner . . . and at night there are the nice little rooms emerging one by one from the big dormitory.[*18*]

The welcoming words of Agassiz to students, faculty, and visiting dignitaries at the opening of the Penikese school were illustrative of his popular concept of nature study. That opening on schedule had itself been made possible because Agassiz had pleaded with the workmen to labor on a Sunday since the work they did, he affirmed, was of a higher order of virtue than keeping the Lord's day, one in congruence with the spiritual values of nature study. The first faculty and that original band of inspired students would later comprise the leaders of natural-history teaching and research well into the early twentieth century. This scientific group, including Nathaniel S. Shaler, William Keith Brooks, Lydia Shattuck, David Starr Jordan, Burt G. Wilder, Alpheus S. Packard, François de Pourtalès, and Alexander Agassiz, was in itself testimony to the posthumous influence of Agassiz and Penikese.

Such men of power and influence who honored the occasion by their presence—James A. Garfield, Joseph
Henry, and Oliver Wendell Holmes—symbolized Agassiz's social force in gaining ends he deemed valuable
for the progress of science. Agassiz instructed the heter-
ogeneous assemblage as to their mission and purpose:

> You will find the same elements of instruction all
> about you wherever you may be teaching. You can
> take your classes out, and give them the same lessons,
> and lead them up to the same subjects you are . . .
> studying here. And this mode of teaching . . . is so
> natural, so suggestive, so true. That is the charm of
> teaching from Nature herself. No one can warp her
> to suit his own views. *She brings us back to absolute
> truth as often as we wander.*[19]

It was this stark appeal to the Ideal Virtue of Nature
as objective truth-giver that made Agassiz a public
Deity of Science. His colleagues knew, of course, that
his mental operations were at once comparative and
rational; he did not separate the head of intellectuality
from the trunk of spirit. Other naturalists, such as
Charles Darwin and James Dwight Dana, also knew
that Agassiz had interpreted the facts of nature as he
subjectively understood them.

While frustrating to his peers, this operation of the
intellect highlighted the subtle appeal of Agassiz as
hero of science. Agassiz's appeal was, simply, that nature, when subjectively interpreted, was being viewed

in accordance with the very reality it ideally epitomized
—a philosophical viewpoint in sharp disagreement
with the ideas of such instrumentalists as Thomas
Henry Huxley or Chauncey Wright, but which ac-
corded very well with the modern neo-Platonism Agassiz had absorbed from such teachers as Georges Cuvier,
and a viewpoint that still pervaded American philosophy and science.[20] This ability to make a grandiose
synthesis of modern science and comfortable meta-
physics was the heart of Agassiz's philosophical success
in a culture torn between the sometimes contradictory
appeals of democratic romanticism and the newer rationalism of modern science. By personifying nature
as a unifying force which, if properly appreciated,
would restore to Americans what they had lost as a
result of the dislocations of materialism and expansion-
ism, Agassiz was able to bridge these philosophies.
Turtles could indeed conquer dynamos; it was this
that made Agassiz's mental set so akin to that of Henry
Adams and his circle.[21]

   In the uncertain, chaotic social and economic milieu
of pre- and post-bellum America, the concept of Nature
as truth-provider offered common man and man of
culture alike both a barrier and a bulwark of physical
and metaphysical certainty. Such bastions were necessary in a world buffeted by the winds of Darwinian
transformation, the forces of social and industrial
change, the dissolution of the old order of conservative
republican virtue, and the growing stench of political

and economic fraud and corruption. Louis Agassiz offered striking physical and psychological evidence of
opposition to the derivative, shoddy aspects of American culture that Adams, Santayana, and Henry James
all deplored. In challenge to the shabbiness of Grant-
ism and expansionist materialism, Agassiz made common cause with his Liberal Republican friends to
conserve the virtue and the nature of America, qualities it had once known and lost in the rococo, gilded
sham of the Age of Excess.

The Penikese venture can be represented as a kind
of pastoral haven where, in the uncertain world of
1872–1874, there existed a place of affirmative value.
Facts replaced fanciful notions, and the validity of
nature made strong-thewed American workmen at one
with men and women scientists who daily went out
from the island's shores or tramped its rocky fields in
search of direct contact with the wholeness of natural
things and their Creator. This species of Penikese appeal sheds light upon the constant American fascination with nature, one that runs like a red thread
through cultural history from the days of the Puritans
through the exploits of Rafinesque, John and William
Bartram, John James Audubon, Agassiz, Whitman,
John Muir, Luther Burbank, and Theodore Roosevelt.
It also helps to explicate the national fascination with
nature study in contrast to the neutrality or hostility
felt by various publics to the physical sciences.

The Penikese picnic, experiment, and vision took

place at the very time when Ulyssess S. Grant, having just taken the oath of presidential office for the second time, had been found directly and indirectly responsible for vast land frauds in the trans-Mississippi West, the notorious peculations in the departments of Interior, War, and the Treasury, and the involvement of Vice-President Schuyler Colfax in the use of government monetary power to aid special corporate interests. The result was elitist disenchantment with the politics of the age, a sentiment that led such friends of Agassiz as Charles Francis Adams to form the Liberal Republican movement as a countervailing force to the burgeoning political and economic corruption. Given the situation of our own time, history offers us a pessimistic analogy with conditions one hundred years ago. The vibrant summers at Penikese Island can seem to present-day observers, as they did to Brahmins and fledgling teachers—as a necessary and virtuous barrier between nature the truth-giver and society, seen as Henry Adams' dynamo, a perpetual value-less, expansionist machine, like an engine out of control, that man's technology had created but could not stop.

Agassiz's affirmation of the salvation achievable through direct contact with nature was in harmony with the ideas of those long-viewing men who sat down with him once each month at Boston's Saturday Club, and planned radical forays into the realms of science, politics, and culture to salvage the American condition. Holmes, Lowell, Sumner, Longfellow, Edward P.

Whipple, Samuel Gridley Howe, Thomas G. Appleton, and Agassiz comprised, with other men of similar quality, a coterie of what might be termed *republican radicals* whose desires, while sometimes differing on details and issues, were common; to turn back the clock on the age of gilt and restore the virtues of the noble past. Jefferson would readily have understood this historical radicalism. Of these men, Agassiz was a major figure because he alone embodied the attributes of science, cosmopolitanism, genteel culture, and ease in company with common and cultured man alike. Fanny Longfellow's judgment of the Saturday Club aggregation is revealing: "they are too busy, or too domestic, and hardly one of them but Agassiz is to be relied on for any social purposes."[22] Those social talents, so clearly recognized by Lyman, made Penikese possible.

The first American summer school for natural history study was much more than a training ground for teachers of science. It was a composite of long-visioned leadership, dedicated workers in the vineyard of science, male and female co-existence on an entirely novel scale, financed by old wealth, and made ultimately possible by the steam engine that was Agassiz. Agassiz took this task, as he did others at the first blush of enthusiastic inception, with high seriousness and devotion, and marshalled all the social, political, and economic resources at his command. A wealthy Bostonian donated his yacht for offshore dredging; Agassiz's col-

league and friend of many years, United States Coast
Survey Director Benjamin Peirce, made the necessary
equipment for offshore dredging freely available. A
band of dedicated former students who included Alex
Agassiz, Nathaniel S. Shaler, Addison E. Verrill, Alpheus Hyatt, Frederick Ward Putnam, Pourtalès, and
Alpheus S. Packard were recruited for the first faculty.
A national search for qualified students was begun,
and, of the more than three hundred applications received, it was possible to accept only fifty, of whom
thirty-five were men and fifteen women. Many of
these went on to notable careers in science; David Starr
Jordan, later to become Stanford's president and a fine
diplomat in the nation's service, met his wife there
that summer—the young biologist apparently taking
most seriously the Agassiz dictum to "study nature not
books."*[23]*

The image that Agassiz was careful to impress regarding dedication to empirical nature study was exemplified by the no-nonsense approach he adopted
toward these students who braved the inconveniences
of life in the field. Because of delays in dormitory construction, these were, male and female budding *savants*
alike, just barely segregated from each other by hastily
thrown-together walls. Six spirited youths took the
opportunity to play a sporting prank on the young
women bedded nearby, and, when Agassiz heard of it,
he immediately told them to leave the island. This action, typical of Agassiz's determination to see nature

study undertaken seriously, was virtually sanctified by a kind of religious dedication that tended to preclude occupation with the material or the worldly aspects of life. Two evidences of the natural religiosity that this Penikese venture inspired will suffice. The first is from John Greenleaf Whittier's *The Prayer of Agassiz,* celebrating that first day at Penikese:

> On the isle of Penikese,
> Ringed about by sapphire seas,
> Fanned by breezes salt and cool,
> Stood the Master with his school . . .
> Said the Master to the Youth:
> "We have come in search of truth,
> Trying with uncertain key
> Door by door of mystery;
> We are reaching through His laws,
> To the garment-hem of Cause . . .
> We are groping here to find . . .
> What the Thought which underlies
> Nature's masking and disguise,
> What it is that hides beneath
> Blight and bloom and birth and death . . .
> Doubt and error, loss and failing,
> Of our weakness made aware . . ."
>
> Then the Master in his place
> Bowed his head a little space,
> And the leaves by soft airs stirred
> Lapse of wave, and cry of bird . . .

Even the careless heart was moved,
And the doubting gave assent...
To the Master well-beloved...
All who gazed upon him saw...
How his face was still uplit...
Hopeful, trustful, full of cheer,
And the love that casts out fear.*[24]*

The second illustration is from the recollections of
the naturalist David Starr Jordan, who, like the poet,
was similarly moved to record the occasion, giving his
report of Agassiz's first talk to students and faculty on
the day after the opening ceremonies:

Breakfast over, Agassiz . . . spoke . . . of his purpose
in calling us together. The swallows flew in and out
of the building . . . Some grazed his shoulder as he
dwelt with intense earnestness on the needs of the
people for truer education—needs that could be met
by the training and consecration of devoted teachers. This was to him no ordinary school . . . still less
a mere summer's outing, but a missionary work of
the highest importance. A deep religious feeling
permeated his whole discourse, for in each natural
object he saw a "thought of God" which the student
may search out and think over again . . . At the end
he said . . . "I would not have anyone pray for me
now" adding . . . that each would frame his own
prayer in silence.*[25]*

Whittier had written his poem and prayer, and, with respect to Pound's admiration of Agassiz's precision in prose, I merely suggest that the Penikese experience, while important for science and culture, probably yielded more mawkish poetry by amateur and established writers than New England had known in her cultural history. But Agassiz did inspire sentimentality and overblown romanticization. As William James, Edward S. Morse, Artemus Ward, and Josh Billings demonstrated in prose and picture, Agassiz was a perfect subject for the duality of admiration and satire. To be the subject of caricature, or to inspire the appellation Asa Gray bestowed, *Agassizzia Suavis,* a man must also be worthy of secret or overt admiration, even by those who find fault with him. The fulfillment of the Penikese idea was made possible by the syncretism of those broad, colorful, and overly enthusiastic aspects of Agassiz's personality with the New England virtues of energy and dedication to one's fellow man that Agassiz also exemplified.

A fine example of this fusion is found in the words recorded by an anonymous Penikese student in his diary during that first summer of 1873:

A student at Penikese found an egg in the body of a skate he was dissecting. When this was shown to Agassiz, he was highly interested and excited, stating that no human eye had ever seen this. He nervously

dissected the fish, and found instead two eggs, say-
ing: "Truly . . . the sight of these two eggs alone
would pay me for my whole summer's work!" When
the eggs were exposed, Agassiz was very excited say-
ing, "I would not take two thousand dollars for that
rare specimen. No human eye but ours has ever seen
it. I would not exchange it for the Madonna of
Raphael!"*[26]*

It is hard to imagine a young naturalist failing to be
kindled by the enthusiasm of an individual who could,
with ease, equate a discovery in science with a work of
high aesthetic creation.

It should be emphasized that, although students of
Agassiz such as Morse found his dominance occasion-
ally intolerable, they were also awed by the beauty of
his better self, during his lifetime and especially after
his death, when the process of historiographic webspin-
ning began. A good example of this double vision is
found in the observations of William James, who, at
twenty-three, was chosen as one of those Harvard students of science fortunate enough to accompany Agassiz and Lizzie on the Brazilian expedition of 1865–
1866.

Writing to his father, Henry James the elder, the
naturalist-in-training observed of himself and his
teacher:

I said to myself before I came away: "W. J. in this
excursion you'll learn to know yourself and your re-

sources as some what more intimately than you do now, and will come back with your character considerably evolved and established."

This was the effect Agassiz had on many bright young men, calling forth the best that was in them, and urging introspection as to how they would spend their time and, indeed, their lives. So boundless was his own energy, he would not tolerate what he felt to be sloth or needless inactivity. James understood this. "I am now certain that my *forte* is not to go on [an] exploring expedition . . . before starting out . . . I was so filled with . . . the romance of the thing [but] here . . . the romance vanishes and the misgivings float up."[27] James's dislike for nature study may have lost zoology a devotee but gained much for the progress of psychology and philosophy. Those qualities of young James's mind are revealed in his estimate of Agassiz the person:

> Agassiz . . . is an extraordinary being, having with all his foibles a greater personal fascination than anyone I know.[28]

This estimate by a young man with James's affiliations in New England elite culture makes more believable the awe of the young Penikese student and the admiration of Henry Adams. That admiration comprised not merely intellectual respect, but the idealization of the scholar-as-activist that captured the imagination of such men as Thoreau, Emerson, Lowell, and Theodore

Roosevelt. Thoreau delighted in the equality he knew through intellectual and personal association, as the two men exchanged information and specimens on turtles indigenous to the Concord region. Emerson exulted in the sallies at the Saturday Club, wrote Agassiz letters of high admiration, and accompanied him and Longfellow on a trip to the White Mountains. In Brazil, William James soon found that his original impression of nature study was not entirely correct, because, under Agassiz's tutelage:

> now that the real enjoyment of the expedition is beginning, and I am tasting the sweets of these lovely forests . . . I find it impossible to tear myself away and this morning told the Prof. that I would see this Amazon trip through . . . I see . . . a chance of learning a good deal of Zoology and botany . . . and I am getting a pretty valuable training from the Prof. who pitches into me right and left and makes me [own] up to a great many of my imperfections. This morning he said I was "totally uneducated." *[29]*

James was learning what other students would soon learn during that Penikese summer: that personal dedication to science yielded an incomparable education, pre-eminent because of the intense dedication of The Master. The founder of pragmatism could thus confide to his father:

> I have profited a great deal by hearing Agassiz talk. Not so much by what he says for never did a man

utter a greater amount of humbug but by learning the way of feeling of such a vast practical engine as he is. No one sees farther into a generalization than his own knowledge of details extends, and you have a greater feeling of weight and solidity about the presence of this great background of special facts than about the mind of any other man I know. He has a great personal tact, too, and I see that . . . he is pitching into my loose and superficial way of thinking. I have said a great deal against him which if repeated to strangers w[oul]d generate an impression that I disliked him very much. That is not at all the case . . . Now that I am become more intimate with him and can talk more freely to him, I delight to be with him. I only saw his defects at first, but now his wonderful qualities throw them quite into the background. . . . I never saw a man work so hard. Physically, intellectually and socially he has done the work of ten different men . . . *[30]*

Of all The Master's contemporary analysts, James came nearest to cutting through the tangle behind the tangle. His effort, as with any desire to reach to the heart of a subject, could not fail to result in respect and even appreciation for the object of study. The unequivocal social and physical impression Agassiz made shines vividly in James's observations:

The Professor has just been expatiating over the mass of South America and making projects as if he

had Sherman's Army at his disposal instead of the
ten novices he really has . . . The Prof. now sits opposite me with his face all aglow holding forth . . .
about the imperfect education of the American people . . . *Offering* your services to Agassiz is as absurd
as it w[oul]d [be] for a S[outh] Carolinian to *invite*
Gen. Sherman's soldiers to partake of some refresh-
ment when they called at his house.*[31]*

Thirty years later, James, now an established man of
letters, gave a memorial address on Agassiz. His words
provide a fascinating counterpoint to the reflections of
the twenty-three-year-old student. There is little sense
of sentimental hero worship, but rather an appraisal of
Agassiz that, in 1896, gave a view rather typical of those
who knew him intimately in the years of Penikese:

The secret of such an extraordinary effective influence lay in the equally extraordinary mixture of the
animal and social gifts, the intellectual powers, and
the desires and passions of the man . . . His passion
for knowing living things was combined with a rapid-
ity of observation, and a capacity to recognize them
again and remember everything about them . . . If
ever a person lived by faith, he did . . . The secret of
it all was, that while his scientific ideals were an in-
tegral part of his being, so that wherever he went he
came forward as "the Professor" and talked "shop"
to every person, young or old, great or little, learned
or unlearned . . . he was at the same time so com-

manding a presence, so curious and inquiring, so responsive and expansive, so generous and reckless of himself, that every one said immediately "here . . . is a man on the heroic scale, not to serve whom is avarice and sin." He elevated the popular notion of what a student of Nature should be. . . . He was a splendid example of the temperament that looks forward and not backward, and never wastes a moment in regrets for the irrevocable . . . as we look back on Agassiz, there floats up a breath of life's morning, that makes the world seem young and fresh once more.*[32]*

So vital was Agassiz's individuality that the philosopher of empiricism—a credo totally different from that system of belief in the Platonic special creationism that Agassiz espoused—ranked his heroic qualities as those of a man ahead of his time, whose example was of the sort to lead Americans back from the degradation of democracy in the post-Civil War era.

The goal of explaining the true meaning of Agassiz's love affair with the teaching of natural history must be viewed as one of comprehending the dedication of a romantic who would literally abjure the Madonna if he could turn Americans to the simple, Godly virtues of real and ideal connection with organic creation. As Adams was to do, Agassiz realistically and metaphorically urged his countrymen to recapture the Walden Ponds of the imagination created for them by Jefferson, Thoreau, and Emerson. Penikese Island instruction may have lasted but two summers; its inspirer, in the minds of some colleagues, may have lacked scientific superiority, but its prominence bares significant traits of national culture.

The Penikese experiment was a microcosm of Agassiz's life in science, an experience that conjoined the research emphasis of his European career with the public aspects more dominant in his American life. That life was remarkable for Agassiz's role as a catalyst, moving private and public men to finance large scientific projects in large-minded ways. During his lifetime, Agassiz was responsible for securing nearly one million dollars for the study of natural history.[33] This amount, moreover, does not include sums given him, his students, and his assistants by the United States Coast Survey, the Smithsonian Institution, the United States Fish Commission, and various government exploring organizations. If Agassiz's social grace and power aroused the jealousy of colleagues such as William Barton Rogers or Asa Gray, it delighted the mass of Americans in many stations of life. They paid to hear his public lectures on such subjects as glacial history or embryology, underwrote the costs of research and publication, made possible professorships and research facilities, financed the Museum of Comparative Zoology, and, among other signs of esteem, made viable the Thayer Expedition, the *Hassler* cruise, and the Anderson School and Penikese Island station.

Until recently, historians have espoused a view that claimed antipathy between the predominantly *laissez faire* world of business, industry, and finance and the public support of cultural and intellectual life. Government and private monies, they asserted, did not exert a positive influence in funding intellectual life. The inner history of American culture from the 1840s through the 1890s and the special development of science in America offer direct contradiction to these assumptions.[34] They were assumptions grounded on the web-spinning of men such as Adams, who affirmed that America had nothing to contribute to the life of the intellect, and were then, ironically, reinforced by populist historians of the 1930s. Those historians, accepting this assumption, blamed it on the dominance of anti-intellectual industrial social psychology, thus doing their share to construct myths consonant with those of the earlier elitists whom they apparently despised.[35]

In actuality, scholars of Agassiz's day saw no distinction in seeking support for their endeavors from any source. That support, whether from the private or public sector, was welcomed in science, if its use was defined by scientists themselves, if the money was given without expectation of either immediate benefit or psychological feelings of the expiation of guilt. Agassiz, Alexander Dallas Bache, Joseph Henry, John Wesley Powell, Alpheus Hyatt, and Albert S. Bickmore (a prime mover in establishing the American Museum of

Natural History) were among the notable men of science whose work was marked by this connection with private and public money. Of all such scientists, Agassiz ranked first. His private donors were noteworthy. They represented a segment of financial power that was, to a great degree, dissociated from the caricature of the late-nineteenth-century *nouveau riche* robber baron so despised in the historiography of the 1930s and 1940s. Men of the caliber of Jay Gould, Jim Fiske, or Andrew Carnegie, did not figure in the coterie of Agassiz backers. Even a partial listing of Agassiz's rich benefactors reveals that they were wealthy New Englanders or New Yorkers, whose money came from the older forms of trade and commerce that had provided the economic bases for the earlier happy republic that Henry Adams inhabited in spirit. Hence, John Amory Lowell (who first brought Agassiz to America), Francis Calley Gray (the angel of the *Contributions*), Nathaniel Thayer (supporter of the Harvard Museum and the Brazil venture), Theodore Lyman, Quincy Adams Shaw, and Henry Lee Higginson (these last related to Agassiz by marriage) were all men of the class of Henry Adams and his father Charles Francis Adams, who believed in the older republican virtues. These consisted of the wise governance of society by men of money and power and of a land whose future resided in the intelligent concentration of resources in culture, politics, and the idea of selfless service to one's fellow men. There

was no distinction between the efforts of a John Amory
Lowell to bring Agassiz to America to lecture on natural history at the institute for public education that
bore his name and the efforts of John Anderson. They
sized the opportunity, by supporting nature's study
and appreciation, to protest materially against the
shabbiness of America, and the new populism of their
age.

George William Curtis was a noted Brahmin who
gave a characteristic advocacy to this concept. In 1877
he voiced his views:

> By . . . public duty I mean . . . that constant and ac-
> tive practical participation . . . without which . . . the
> conduct of public affairs falls under the control of
> selfish and ignorant, or crafty and venal men . . . To
> say that in this country the rogues must rule, is to
> defy history and to despair of the republic . . . Great
> genius and force of character undoubtedly make
> their own career. . . . so deep is the conviction that
> sooner or later madness . . . must seize every repub-
> lic [that] . . . it is indeed a master passion, but its con-
> trol *is the true conservation of the republic and of
> happy human progress;* and it is men made familiar
> by education . . . It is . . . necessary for us to perceive
> the vital relation of individual courage and character
> to the common welfare . . .it is of . . . importance that
> we choose to do what is wise and right.*[36]*

It is quite credible to imagine Agassiz, at a meeting of the Saturday Club, listening with strong concurrence to words such as these from Curtis:

> In America . . . New England has inspired and moulded our national life. But if New England has led the Union, what has led New England? Her scholarly class . . . with the rest; men of strong convictions and persuasive speech, who showed their brethren what they ought to think and do. That is the secret of leadership. It is not servility to the mob . . . Leadership is the power of kindling a sympathy and trust which will eagerly follow . . . As educated America was the constructive power, so it is still the true conservative force of the Republic . . . Take from the country . . . its educated power, and you would take . . . from national action its moral mainspring.*[37]*

No words express more succinctly Agassiz's role as conduit between cultivated and common man.

By analogy, it was as if Agassiz had become a natural history money depository which would transform wealth into the moral equivalent of the virtues of love, work, and fellowship. Americans could thus feel strong and renewed by giving succor to an Agassiz adventure in furtherance of the good olden virtues of closeness to nature, sacredness of fact, and truth through beauty. This was the chemistry that linked the mechanic at his Lyceum lectures with the men who paid money to make Agassiz's addresses possible, a congruence rarely understood in efforts to analyze democratic culture. The values that Agassiz stood for were romanticized into a religion of nature that witnessed women of the 1850s holding live grasshoppers in their hands, and their daughters of the 1870s striding out to the marshes and offshore waters of Penikese, sketching pad in hand, collector's box at the ready, prepared to take the field in the cause of virtuous science.

With the shield of "study nature not books" held high, Agassiz would also help to advance cultural life in America by relating science to ideal goals of education and civilization virtuous in and for themselves, associate preservation and conservation with moral as well as environmental purposes, and thus preserve Penikese and Cape Cod from the metaphorical rapine of a Jay Gould. The affiliation of Miss Cary, Agassiz, and John Anderson would contradict assertions of conflict between popular democracy and leadership by a self-elected elite.

Agassiz, his friends, and their decendants were indeed an intellectual and cultural elite who employed both money and popular and establishment approval to gain their special goals. But this elite strove for ends that, as Curtis affirmed, were ideally necessary for advanced civilization. At an earlier time, these goals had been directed toward the creation of a self-governing group of scientists and their lay allies whose purposes were the control of private and government science, higher education, and the directions of power and decision making in the worlds of ideas and values. Agassiz, Benjamin Peirce, Cornelius Conway Felton, Alexander Dallas Bache, and other men of letters, politics, and science called themselves "scientific Lazzaroni" or, in their view, beggars who worked in common cause to gain from Americans that influence which was the inherent right of the distinguished man of letters.[38]

In the case of Penikese, Agassiz used the same means that had been markedly successful on many other occasions to gain large ends. Since 1874, he had longed for a marine biological station where he could study and teach marine biology. From then until 1873, he steadily progressed toward this goal, his appetite whetted by the incredible treasures of marine life offered by America's coasts and made physically available through the assistance of such benefactors as Bache, Peirce, and Thayer. Between 1849 and 1873, scores of papers analyzing and describing American marine biology came from Agassiz's pen, and the facts he discovered were employed in his system of classification that comprised parts of the *Contributions to the Natural History of the United States.*[39] Students of the caliber of Morse, Hyatt, Verrill, Scudder, Jordan, Brooks, and Alex Agassiz all made their reputations in marine biology— a field which exceeded all other specialities in contributions of Agassiz-trained naturalists. The fact that all these men were involved in the Penikese enterprise alone makes it a unique venture in the annals of American natural history.

The establishment of the Anderson School was almost prefigured by Agassiz's success in gaining support for a marine research station on the Charles River, a seaside laboratory begun at Nahant in 1855, and the explorations undertaken with the assistance of François de Pourtalès in the Gulf Stream in 1867–1869. In the meantime, the origin, launching, and success of the Museum of Comparative Zoology at Harvard College made subsequent events the natural consequences of Agassiz's awesome dominance over the culture of natural history in America. That pre-eminence is revealed in a letter written to Agassiz in 1863 by Oliver Wendell Holmes, confidant, friend, and fellow Saturday Club member:

I look with ever increasing admiration on the work you are performing for our civilization. It very rarely happens that the same person can take at once the largest and deepest scientific views and come down without apparent effort to the level of popular intelligence. This is what singularly fits you for our country. . . . You have gained the heart of our purpose . . . and you are setting up a standard . . . which will gradually lift the students of Nature among us to its own level in aspiration.*[40]*

This admixture of genteel admiration and educational philosophy made the Penikese venture an inevitable flowering of the variegated aspects of Agassiz's career in the United States. The combination of teaching, research, discipleship, and national publicity all coalesced, in Agassiz's ever-fertile imagination, to give rise to Penikese—the inevitable result of nearly three decades of work in American natural science and popular education.

Agassiz's purposes in establishing Penikese were multifaceted. Spencer Fullerton Baird, Assistant Secretary of the Smithsonian Institution, Director of the United States Fish Commission since 1871, founder of what would become the United States National Museum, and an ichthyologist of more than average distinction, faced personal and political problems with the founding of the Anderson School. Agassiz had been instrumental in gaining Baird's appointment to the Smithsonian. Because of his standing as an intimate friend of Smithsonian Secretary Joseph Henry and as a Regent of the Institution since 1863, Agassiz came to assume a proprietary interest in and control over ichthyological specimens collected for and housed at the Washington science center. This behavior ultimately annoyed Baird, especially Agassiz's practice of sending students like Shaler, Hyatt, and Putnam to Washington to bring back original specimens for the Harvard museum. Feeling isolated, Baird turned to Agassiz's enemies, William Barton Rogers and Asa Gray, for support in the game of science politics. This resulted in Baird's election to the Lazzaroni-inspired National Academy of Sciences, after a bitter battle.*[41]*

Formal cordiality and research cooperation now seemed to characterize the two men's relations. However, Baird's developing interest in advanced marine biology, coming at a time when Agassiz's wide-ranging activities made it difficult to concentrate on any single task, posed a strong threat to the latter's dominance. Baird had started research at Woods Hole and the surrounding islands as early as 1863; his interests were marine biological research and, more specifically, the marine ecology of the Cape Cod area. He had begun to lobby independently with legislators for establishment of the United States Fish Commission, to serve the aims of his modern approach to natural history. Acting from this power base, Baird started a Woods Hole research station, and told Agassiz of his immediate and long-range plans for the Fish Commission, especially in regard to Cape Cod ecology.

On Agassiz's return from the *Hassler* cruise in December of 1872, The Master proceeded to outflank this power play on the part of a mere amateur at the game. He adopted the plan for a summer natural history school developed by his student, Nathaniel S. Shaler, and announced in a brochure of December 14, 1872, that it was to be headquartered on Nantucket Island. Agassiz then gained the sympathy of James Abram Garfield, an influential Ohio Congressman and himself a semiprofessional naturalist. The Master's skill is plain in this excerpt from Garfield's diary:

> Dined at . . . [Congressman Samuel] Hooper's with Professor Agassiz and . . . Professor [Benjamin] Peirce. I know of few characters more simple and grand than Professor Agassiz. He carries all the sweetness of childhood in his nature with the strength and massiveness and grandeur of a great man. He has invited me to spend part of the summer at Nantucket Island where he and other scientific men are to lecture to teachers. I shall be glad to accept . . .*[42]*

With the aid of Massachusetts' Congressman Hooper —a key Agassiz political ally—Agassiz next approached the Massachusetts General Court. He had recently resumed his former post on the State Board of Agriculture, the better to convince legislators of the practical value of natural history. At the same time, the circular advertising the Nantucket summer school for natural history was widely distributed, so that, by March of 1873, Agassiz had prepared the ground for possible state funding, monies he had readily commanded for the Museum of Comparative Zoology even in 1871–72, a time of severe fiscal stringency. Baird, aware of the inexorable flow of events, now readily agreed to teach on the faculty of the new school, and Agassiz took the occasion of the annual museum visit by the legislature

in March to ask financing for the summer school concept. His wife recounted the occasion:

> Agassiz laid this new project before them as one of
> deep interest for science in general, and . . . for
> schools and colleges . . . He considered it also an ed-
> ucational branch of the Museum, having, as such, a
> claim on their sympathy, since it was in the line of
> the direct growth and continuance of the same work.
> Never did he plead more eloquently . . .*[43]*

It could not have been mere coincidence that Agassiz's
words were printed in the New York papers the fol-
lowing day, and, even before the solons had time to
consider or act on Agassiz's plea, there came a telegram
and a personal emissary from Anderson to Agassiz. The
deeding of Penikese and its buildings and the gift of
$50,000.00 followed in breathtaking succession.*[44]*
Baird could do nothing else but assure Agassiz the full
assistance of the Fish Commission; he began an exchange of specimens and ideas concerning modern
marine biological studies with the man whose Smithsonian activities had grated upon him ten years earlier.
Baird could be identified as the physical founder of
the current Marine Biological Station at Woods Hole;
but the Penikese idea, brought to modern realization
with the founding of Woods Hole through the work
of Alpheus Hyatt, William Keith Brooks, and Charles
Otis Whitman in 1888—Agassiz faculty and students

at Penikese—was quite correctly symbolized in the bronze tablet erected on the island at the time of the fiftieth anniversary of the summer school:

In commemoration of
the Anderson School of Natural History
. . .
by
Jean Louis Rodolphe Agassiz . . .
The Marine Biological Laboratory
The Direct Descendant of the Penikese School
Erects This Tablet

This achievement of an Agassiz inspiration had another, less happy consequence. Baird had written him a few days after the close of the summer session:

> I looked upon your experiment at Penikese with great solicitude, not as to its success, because of that I felt assured, but of its influence upon your own health. I sincerely trust you may not have overworked yourself . . . and that after the present fatigue is past you will be the better for it.[45]

Baird's wish was not realized. On December 14, 1873, just one year after the first summer school circular had been printed, Agassiz was dead. The Massachusetts legislature, as if to atone for its remission of duty, appropriated $100,000.00 to the Museum for 1873–1874, and Agassiz's son-in-law, Quincy Adams Shaw, matched this sum with a gift of equal amount, placing The Master at the top of the list of men who raised money for the advance of science in America.

In terms of the need felt by Agassiz and his associates to reinvigorate the national culture, other motives behind the establishment of Penikese must be delineated. The American Civil War unleashed in Agassiz a patriotism that made him even more fiercely devoted to showing the world that national culture was vibrant and progressive, uninfluenced by Southern disunity, populist expansion, or moral shabbiness. He was aware also, as his motives for taking the *Hassler* journey reveal, that the world of scientific advance was passing him by, and that he had perhaps become isolated from modern currents in biology.

Beginning at least as early as 1871, Agassiz had been in correspondence with a young German biologist, Anton Dohrn. In collaboration with Baird, he had helped this naturalist by offering suggestions regarding Dohrn's conception of a Marine Biological Station at Naples in 1870. He also provided instructions for collecting and preserving marine specimens.[46] Dohrn's station, grounded upon the German's idea of a central research establishment housing marine scientists from all over the world, elicited considerable excitement and praise from the scientific community.[47] In his career, Agassiz had usually been generous in sharing knowledge and giving direction to men younger than he; but by the 1870s a curiously altered pattern became plain. When such people appeared capable of striking out on their own and either imitating or superseding Agassiz-styled institutions or scientific innovations, The Master quite often reacted with hostility. The passions aroused by such controversies were intense, and some still remain shrouded in confusion and misunderstanding. The clearest example, however, is the case of Frederick Ward Putnam, Edward S. Morse, Alpheus Hyatt, and Caleb Cooke, who left Agassiz's Museum in 1867 and established the Essex Institute for the promotion of scientific studies in Salem, Massachusetts; at the same time they founded the *American Naturalist,* a periodical that soon became the first professional journal of its kind in the United States.

Although Dohrn had begun the organization of the Naples establishment in November of 1870, he had yet to gain financing, plan buildings, or secure the assistance of governments and research scientists. The Franco-Prussian war made European scientific cooperation difficult, so that, as late as the fall of 1872, the success of Dohrn's activity was not at all assured. Agassiz, who had become by this time very much an American in spirit, could readily hope to outpace the German scientist, and the somewhat frenzied efforts The Master undertook to begin Penikese did indeed ensure its primacy, as Dohrn was unable formally to open his headquarters until February of 1874.

As regards Dohrn's Naples marine biological sta-

tion, Agassiz was resolute in his determination to out-
shine and surpass what Europe had begun. The advancement of research was a basic motive in founding
Penikese. Because Agassiz had fostered an attitude of
the romance of nature, it was unlikely that he could
gain support solely for pure research. The Museum of
Comparative Zoology, for example, was heralded as
both a research and a teaching institution. But to com-
bine these aims would at once secure the primary
goal and satisfy the definition of natural history that
Brahmin and commoner alike had always identified
with Agassiz's efforts. After receiving Anderson's lar-
gesse, Agassiz revealed his intentions to Baird in a
frank letter—plans quite at variance with the summer
school lark Miss Cary reported, or those revealed to
readers of the *New York Tribune* who saw daily ac-
counts of the Penikese lectures in its pages.*[48]*

Baird learned,

I am giving as much time as I possibly can to the
organization of . . . Penikese . . . It is to be a sister
institution of the Museum of Comparative Zoology,
to work hand in hand with it; in fact to stand as the
Educational Branch of the Museum, with an Independent Estate. Instead of being organized as a
Summer School only, Mr. Anderson has consented
to make it a general School of Natural History with
a summer session on Penikese and a winter session
in Cambridge. We must now look to the founding of

ten or twelve regular professorships covering the whole range of the natural sciences, with special reference to their practical application to Agriculture, the Industrial Arts, Medicine, as well as to the progress of science itself. I am now working at the plans for laboratories so that we may from the beginning make experiments upon every question bearing upon the breeding of stock, the raising of fish, bees, silkworms, oysters, lobsters . . . while our students shall be taught what they ought to know in order to teach successfully . . . I depend upon you to advise me as to the best mode of securing daily a large supply of fresh specimens of fish, mollusks, crustacea, etc., as it will be necessary for each pupil to have a specimen of some kind before him, in place of books, which I shall completely exclude from the working rooms.*[49]*

Ezra Pound would have been pleased to read words that gave a further nobility to the virtue of studying the thing-in-itself. In terms of American pedagogy, it is astonishingly modern, even one hundred years afterward, to learn of an idea so boldly innovative: a University would have a permanent branch and the enrichment of a summer setting physically distant but intellectually related; the work of the main institution could thus be carried forward, in different ways, the year round. Marine biological stations that followed Penikese did in fact maintain some form of association with universities or other permanent institutions and communities, so that Agassiz's idea yielded at least partial results for the progress of science. These, however, were sometimes short-lived, because they were presided over by shortsighted men.

Despite the aspect of the plan that publicized summer nature study for schoolteachers, Agassiz was quite candid with John Anderson as to his primary desires. He employed the same formula whereby he had made the Museum of Comparative Zoology at once independent of and also integrated with the structure of Harvard University. "I think it advisable," he wrote to Anderson,

> not to connect the endowment with any State or university . . . but to allow the School the greatest independence . . . I should, however, wish it to be associated with the Museum of Comparative Zoology in such a way as to share at once and forever in any advantages to be derived from an institution so kindred in its . . . aims. These two establishments for the study of natural history will . . . work together to the greatest advantage of both . . . and I should wish that the terms of any settlement about the landed property and the income should not limit the working of the School to the summer months only, but include the idea of continuing its operations in connection with the Museum in Cambridge during the whole year. We have rich and extensive

collections [there] which may be made of infinite
service to the School we are about to establish...*[50]*

Agassiz's wishes were readily acceptable to Anderson.
It is of note that the great outpouring of romantic
panegyrical memorabilia, quasi history, and official ac-
counts of the establishment of the Anderson School
and the Woods Hole Marine Biological Laboratories
from 1873 until the present time fails to mention this
notable aspect of Agassiz's plan for progressive natural
science—this, despite the fact that Agassiz's letter to
Anderson was printed in the official *Report* of the
Board of Trustees recounting the events of the first
two summers at Penikese.*[51]* One may reasonably
conclude that American scientists who wrote their his-
tories in the years since the 1870s found it more grati-
fying to recount with sentimentality every exciting and
uplifting Penikese story, thus blinding us to the reality
of what was attempted in those notable summers on
Cape Cod.

Agassiz's ability to sharpen the sword of scientific
politics to a fine edge to achieve his purposes, revealed
in his letter to Anderson—and many others like it—
should underscore the fact that the new scientist had
to excel in diplomatic, political, and social skills as
well as intellectual brilliance in order to gain the opportunity to attempt cultural transformation.

Agassiz may, therefore, be classed as a truly modern
prototype, for his students learned these lessons from

him and from other men in different humanistic and social scientific realms who consciously followed the model he established. In the instance of Agassiz's image of what Penikese would be, it is plain that he wanted to create an institution superior to Dohrn's Naples station, just as he constantly heralded the Harvard Museum as soon to be the equal of France's *Jardin des Plantes*. Agassiz patently felt that it would be worthwhile to inform Dohrn of his democratization of research science. Just before Penikese began operations, he told the young German savant:

> It is a great pleasure and satisfaction that I can tell you how, in consequence of the munificence of a wealthy New York merchant, it has become *my duty* to erect an establishment whose main *object will be similar to that of your Naples station, only that teaching* is to be united with it . . . a sum of $50,000.00 was *handed over to me* and now I am erecting . . . a school of natural history which at the same time will be a zoological station in the immediate neighborhood of the gulf-stream, of the greatest assistance to our zoologists, and especially . . . splendid a dredging ground. This certainly must promote zoological study in the United States.[52]

Two months later, Penikese in full swing, Agassiz wrote to Dohrn about his progress. He detailed the virtues of the physical environment, the nature and construction of the laboratories and experimental stations, and the investigations underway with domestic animals. He ended with words that could not fail to have an impact on a young German dedicated to scientific advance:

> Next year [1874] physical, chemical and physiologi-
> cal laboratories will be constructed . . . I believe I
> did not tell you that my son presented me on my
> birthday with $100,000.00 for the enlargement of
> the Museum. I intend to apply this sum chiefly to
> the augumentation of the collections, hoping the
> state will pay for the enlargement of the build-
> ings.[53]

It is quite understandable that, from the 1860s on, Agassiz was able to attract first-rate European natural- ists to Harvard and also to use private wealth to buy the great collections of impoverished European scien- tists and institutions. This is why French professor- ships, temporary tiffs with fellow scientists, or even the increasing loss of physical vigor did not deter Agas- siz from the belief that the natural resources of America were indeed a virgin land to be placed at the intelligent disposition of civilized men.

That the Penikese dreams did not come to pass in full because Agassiz's physical exertions for American science outstripped his body's ability to cope with them was unimportant. What is notable is that Agassiz's con- cept of Penikese was a prefiguration of what at least in part came to pass in marine biological field study through the efforts of Alpheus S. Packard at the Peabody

Academy, Alpheus Hyatt at Annisquam, Alex Agassiz at Newport, and Whitman and Brooks at Woods Hole during the years 1873 to 1888. The Penikese idea thereby established modern professional marine biology. What has falsely been identified as a summer school of natural history was, in fact, an ideal form that comfortably merged European professionalism, American elitism, and social democracy.

It fell to Alex Agassiz to preside over the immediate death of Penikese. Alex's letters, subsequent to his father's death, expressed poignant hope for what might have been together with practical understanding of what the loss of the steam engine meant to the grand dreams that chugged it ever forward. He vainly tried to raise money, writing to a potential donor:

Professor Agassiz always drew largely upon the fund of Mr. Anderson. His . . . failing health warned him that his time was short, and he felt the importance of establishing the School on a broad and comprehensive basis, both scientific and personal, for professors and students. The school . . . has not only exercised . . . a powerful influence in America, but is recognized abroad wherever an interest is felt in the progress of popular culture. Even Seaside laboratories, lately established in . . . Europe, *have never aimed at the vital and widespread connection with the education of the people which lies at the very foundation of the Anderson school.*[54]

Alex confided to Ernest Haeckel, the naturalist, that:

> I shall try to carry out . . . the many plans regarding
> Penikese and the Museum which were started by my
> father . . . I shall at least have the melancholy satis-
> faction of knowing that in his case at least his views,
> whether right or wrong and his dearest wishes will
> be faithfully executed . . . that I may raise a monu-
> ment to him surpassing what he had hoped to be
> able to do and better perhaps because I shall not
> have the incessant temptation of remodeling as I go
> along.[55]

But history proved Alex wrong in design and intent.
He was forced to economize more and more stringently
so as to deflate and make realistic the vast commitments
his father had made, often without his son's knowledge.
In 1874, Alex Agassiz confessed to Oliver Wolcott
Gibbs, one of that energetic and determined band of
scientific Lazzaroni,

> I was obliged to drop Penikese. It broke me down
> completely . . . all have expressed the utmost grati-
> tude and satisfaction with it, and when I remember
> what chances I had for work when I began, I don't
> wonder at it.[56]

There could not be a more concrete example of the
truth of Theodore Lyman's words that there could
never be a successor to the steam engine that was Agassiz. That engine, in days when the transcontinental

railroads were drawing the nation together physically, had drawn it closer socially and culturally.

It was perhaps a fitting end to the Penikese adventure, one that Henry Adams at least would have chuckled over, that in August of 1873, while still at the island school, Agassiz had received a letter from President Grant and the entire Cabinet, inviting him to visit Washington and lecture on any subject of his choice, so illustrious was his reputation as a world-famed naturalist.[57] Had he been able to accept, Vice-President Colfax might have been enlightened regarding the proper use of natural resources, while the secretaries of the Interior and Treasury departments might have gained some insights into the practice and philosophy of conservation.

In this effort to determine the nature of the whale, keenly aware of the warnings of Auden, Royce, Lowell, Adams, and James who have tried to separate fact from fancy and aspects of the past from their own views of it, the historical concept of still another Brahmin of the republican persuasion is most metaphorically instructive. Henry James's novel, *The Aspern Papers,* included a dialogue between the narrator and Juliana Bordereau in which he strove to persuade her to let him possess the precious manuscripts of Jeffrey Aspern that she controlled: "If you write books, don't you sell them?" Juliana asked of the ostensible man of letters. "I think there is no more money to be made by literature . . . What do you write about?"

"About the books of other people. I'm a critic, an historian, in a small way . . ."

"Do you think it's right to rake up the past?"

"I don't know what you mean by raking it up; but how can we get at it unless we dig a little? The present has such a rough way of treading it down."

"Oh, I like the past, but I don't like the critics . . ."

"Neither do I, but I like their discoveries."

"Aren't they mostly lies?"

"The lies are what they sometimes discover . . . they often lay bare the truth."

"The truth is God's, it isn't man's; we had better leave it alone. Who can judge of it—who can say?" *[58]*

NOTES

1   Quoted in Daniel Aaron, "The Treachery of Recollection: the Inner and the Outer History," in Robert H. Bremner (ed.), *Essays on History and Literature* (Columbus, Ohio: Ohio State University Press, 1966), p. 27.

2   Quoted in Bert James Loewenberg (ed.), *Charles Darwin: Evolution and Natural Selection* (Boston: Beacon Press, 1959), p. 4.

3   (Boston: Houghton Mifflin Company, 1961), p. 4.

4   Ernest Samuels, *The Young Henry Adams* (Cambridge, Mass.: Harvard University Press, 1948); *Henry Adams: The Middle Years* (Cambridge, Mass.: Harvard University Press, 1958); *Henry Adams: The Major Phase* (Cambridge, Mass.: Harvard University Press, 1964); James K. Flack, *Desideratum in Washington: The Intellectual Community in the Capital City, 1870–1900* (Cambridge, Mass.: Schenkman Publishing Company, 1974).

5   (New York: Random House, 1941), pp. 22–23.

6   "Agassiz," *Atlantic Monthly* 33 (May 1874): 586–587, 596. Italics added.

7   Quoted in Guy Davenport (ed.), *The Intelligence of Louis Agassiz* (Boston: Beacon Press, 1963), p. 5.

8   The novel was published anonymously in 1880 by Henry Holt, Inc., in New York. Adams acknowledged authorship in 1907 to a literary historian; Holt announced it publicly in 1921.

9   See *Theodore Roosevelt: An Autobiography* (New York: The Macmillan Company, 1913); *The Winning of the West*, 4 vols.

(New York and London: G. P. Putnam's Sons, 1889–1906); Elting E. Morison and John M. Blum (eds.), *The Letters of Theodore Roosevelt,* 8 vols. (Cambridge, Mass.: Harvard University Press, 1951–54).

10 *Character and Opinion in the United States* (New York: Charles Scribner's Sons, 1921), pp. 1–2.

11 *The Education of Henry Adams* (Boston: Houghton Mifflin Company, 1961), p. 3.

12 27 August 1872, Theodore Lyman Papers, Museum of Comparative Zoology, Harvard University.

13 Quoted in Dorothy G. Wayman, *Edward Sylvester Morse: A Biography* (Cambridge, Mass.: Harvard University Press, 1942), p. 183.

14 *The Education of Henry Adams* (Boston: Houghton Mifflin Company, 1961), p. 60.

15 *A B C of Reading* (London: Faber and Faber, 1951), p. 17.

16 Four vols. (Boston: Little, Brown and Company, 1857–62).

17 See Professor and Mrs. Louis Agassiz, *A Journey in Brazil* (Boston: Ticknor and Fields, 1868).

18 Quoted in Lucy Allen Paton, *Elizabeth Cary Agassiz: A Biography* (Boston and New York: Houghton Mifflin Company, 1919), pp. 169–70.

19 Quoted in Elizabeth Cary Agassiz (ed.), *Louis Agassiz: His Life and Correspondence,* 2 vols. (Boston: Houghton Mifflin Company, 1885), 2: 775. Italics added.

20 See Edward Lurie, *Louis Agassiz: A Life in Science* (Chicago: The University of Chicago Press, 1960), pp. 60–64, 80–84, 252–302.

21 See William Martin Smallwood, *Natural History and the American Mind* (New York: Columbia University Press, 1941); Edward Lurie (ed.), *An Essay on Classification* (Cambridge, Mass.: Harvard University Press, 1962); Edward Waldo Emerson, *The Early Years of the Saturday Club, 1855–1870* (Boston and New York: Houghton Mifflin Company, 1918); Ernest Samuels, *Henry Adams: The Middle Years* (Cambridge, Mass.: Harvard University Press, 1958).

22 Quoted in Martin Duberman, *James Russell Lowell* (Boston: Beacon Press, 1968), p. 192.

23 See David Starr Jordan, *The Days of a Man*, 2 vols. (Yonkers on Hudson, New York: World Book Company, 1922), 2: 106–20, 132.

24 Quoted in Jules Marcou, *Life, Letters, and Works of Louis Agassiz*, 2 vols. (New York: Macmillan and Company, 1896), 2: 203–205.

25 David Starr Jordan, *op. cit.*, 2: 110–11.

26 Quoted in James A. Henshall, "In Memoranium—Louis Agassiz," *Journal of the Cincinnati Society of Natural History* 8 (1885–1886): 139–40.

27 William James [to Henry James, Sr.], 3 June 1865, William James Papers, Houghton Library, Harvard University.

28 *Ibid.*

29 William James [to Henry James, Sr.], 23 August 1865, William James Papers, Houghton Library, Harvard Univerity.

30 William James [to Henry James, Sr.], 12 September 1865, William James Papers, Houghton Library, Harvard University.

31 William James [to his mother], 31 March 1865, William James Papers, Houghton Library, Harvard University.

32 *Louis Agassiz: Words Spoken by Professor William James . . .* (Cambridge, Mass.: [Harvard University], 1897), *passim.*

33 This is a larger estimate than given in my *Louis Agassiz*; it increased as a result of the gifts given during 1872–1874, sums not then known to me.

34 See Edward Lurie, "An Interpretation of Science in the Nineteenth Century: A Study in History and Historiography," *Journal of World History* 7 (1965): 681–706; "Science in American Thought," *Ibid.*: 638–55; "American Scholarship: A Subjective Interpretation of Nineteenth Century Cultural History," in Robert H. Bremner (ed.), *Essays on History and Literature* (Columbus, Ohio: Ohio State University Press), 1966, pp. 31–80; Richard J. Storr, *The Beginnings of Graduate Education in America* (Chicago: The University of Chicago Press, 1953).

35 The best example of this populist history is to be found in

Matthew Josephson, *The Robber Barons; The Great American Capitalists, 1861–1901* (New York: Harcourt, Brace and Company, 1934).

36 "The Public Duty of Educated Men," in Charles Eliot Norton (ed.), *Orations and Addresses of George William Curtis* (New York: Harper and Brothers, 1894), pp. 266, 268, 270, 273, 280. Italics added.

37 "The Leadership of Educated Men," in Norton, *op. cit.,* pp. 323, 326, 331, 335. See also Edwin P. Whipple, *Success and its Conditions* (Boston: J. R. Osgood and Company, 1871).

38 See Edward Lurie, *Louis Agassiz: A Life in Science* (Chicago, The University of Chicago Press, 1960), pp. 182–84, 323–25, 331–34, 360–61, 363.

39 See references in Max Meisel, *Bibliography in American Natural History,* 3 vols. (Brooklyn, New York: The Premier Publishing Company, 1924–1929).

40 20 October 1863, Agassiz Papers, Houghton Library, Harvard University.

41 See Joseph Henry to Agassiz, 13 August 1864, Benjamin Peirce Papers, Harvard University Archives; Agassiz to Joseph Henry, 15 November 1864, Letter Books, 2:125, Museum of Comparative Zoology, Harvard University.

42 17 January 1873. Quoted in Theodore Clarke Smith, *The Life and Letters of James Abram Garfield,* 2 vols. (New Haven: Yale University Press, 1925), 2: 902–903.

43 Elizabeth Cary Agassiz (ed.) *Louis Agassiz: His Life and Correspondence,* 2 vols. (Boston: Houghton Mifflin Company, 1885) 2: 766.

44 *New York Times,* 12 March 1873; *The Organization and Progress of the Anderson School of Natural History* (Cambridge, Mass.: Welch, Bigelow, and Company, 1874), pp. 5–10.

45 27 August 1873, Spencer Fullerton Baird Papers, Smithsonian Institution Archives.

46 Agassiz to Baird, 11 and 18 October 1871, Spencer Fullerton Baird Papers, Smithsonian Institution Archives.

47 See W. A. Herdman, "The Greatest Biological Station in the

World," *The Popular Science Monthly* 48 (September 1901): 419–429; Charles Lincoln Edwards, "The Zoological Station at Naples," *Ibid.* 77 (September 1910): 209–225; "Anton Dohrn," *Science* 36 (October 11, 1912): 453–468).

48 These were printed in permanent form as *Tribune Popular Science: Lectures By L. Agassiz* (Boston and New York: The Tribune Company, 1874).

49 15 April 1873, Spencer Fullerton Baird Papers, Smithsonian Institution Archives.

50 22 March 1873. Quoted in *The Organization and Progress of the Anderson School of Natural History* (Cambridge, Mass.: Welch, Bigelow, and Company, 1874), p. 10.

51 *Ibid.*, pp. 9–10. The most comprehensive history of the subject, Homer A. Jack, "Biological Field Stations of the World," *Chronica Botanica* 9 (Summer 1945), whole number, entirely ignores this aspect of the Anderson School.

52 10 June 1873, in *Nature* 6 (September 25, 1873): 454–55. Italics added.

53 13 August 1873, in *Ibid.*: 455.

54 To [Anon], 15 January 1874, Alexander Agassiz Papers, Museum of Comparative Zoology, Harvard University. Italics added.

55 Museum of Comparative Zoology Letter Books, 5:238, Harvard University.

56 8 August 1874. Quoted in George R. Agassiz (ed.). *Letters and Recollections of Alexander Agassiz* (Boston: Houghton Mifflin Company, 1913), p. 130.

57 6 August 1873, Agassiz Papers, Museum of Comparative Zoology, Harvard University.

58 Two vols. (London and New York: The Macmillan Company, 1888) 1: 147–149.

ILLUSTRATIONS

AND DOCUMENTS

with a

Commentary on

the Letters

Courtesy of the Zinn Collection

1   Louis Agassiz, ca. 1840

2 The first section of the Museum of
Comparative Zoology, 1859

Courtesy of the Zinn Collection

3   Louis Agassiz of Two Minds, ca. 1857

4   America's Student of Nature and
His Material, ca. 1871

Courtesy of the New York Public Library

5   Pencil self-portrait of
William James, ca. 1866

6   Dining Room and Lecture Hall, the Anderson School of Natural History

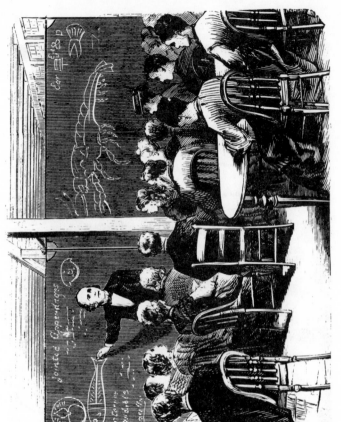

7 Ladies and
Gentlemen
at Nature Study,
the Anderson School
of Natural History

Courtesy of the New York Public Library

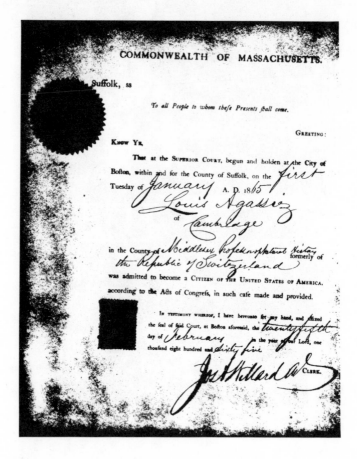

8   Louis Agassiz, a Citizen of
the World—and America

LECTURES

On the successive creation of Organized Beings, fossil and recent,

BY PROF. AGASSIZ,

At the Hall of the University of Pennsylvania,

On the evenings of Tuesday, Thursday and Saturday,

At 7¼ o'clock.

To commence on Tuesday, the 20th inst.

FOR A GENTLEMAN.

Courtesy of the Zinn Collection

Cambridge. Febr. 26. 1871.

My darling Ben,

I am overjoyed at the prospect your letter opens before me. Of course I will go unless Brown Siquard orders me positively to stay on terra firma. But even then I would like to have a hand in arranging the party, as I feel there never was & is not likely soon again to be such an opportunity for promoting the cause of science generally & that of natural History in particular. I would like Pourtalès & Alex to be of the party, & both would delight to join if they possibly can. Pourtalès does not yet know how he will or can arrange his family affairs & Alex though well, dreads the sea. Yet both are as much excited about it as I am, & I have no doubt between us

By permission of the Harvard College Library

Louis Agassiz to Benjamin Peirce
Cambridge, Massachusetts
February 20, 1871

Cambridge, Febr. 20ᵗʰ. 1871.

My darling Ben,

I am overjoyed at the prospect your letter opens before me. Of course I will go unless Brown Séquard orders me positively to stay on terra firma. But even then I would like to have a hand in arranging the party, as I feel there never was and is not likely soon again to be such an opportunity for promoting the cause of science generally & that of Natural History in particular. I would like Pourtalès and Alex [Agassiz] to be of the party & both would delight to join if they possibly can. Pourtalès does not yet know how he will or can arrange his family affairs and Alex though well, dreads the sea. Yet both are as much excited about it as I am; and I have no doubt between us we may organize a working team strong enough to do something creditable. Lizzie is as ever devoted and willing to join in whatever I decide to do.

It seems to me that the best plan to pursue in the survey, would be to select carefully a few points (as many as time would allow) on shore from which to work at right angle with the coast, to as great a distance as the results would justify and then move on to some other headland. And if this plan is adopted it would be desirable to have one additional observer to make collections on shore to connect with the results of the dredgings.

This would be the more necessary, as hardly any thing is known of the shore faunae of the greatest part of S. America, except Brazil. For shore observations I would like a man of the calibre of Dr. Steindachner who has spent a year on the coast of Senegal and would thus bring a knowledge of the opposite side of the Atlantic as a starting Basis of Comparison.

I know [William H.] Dall well enough to be able to say that he is thoroughly qualified to make a zoological survey of Alaska. Whether he could add the geology or not, I do not know. He has one fault, an almost intolerable conceit; but he is very young & may have it rubbed out. He has been so long under the influence of [Spencer Fullerton] Baird that he may not be very friendly to the Museum of Comp.[arative] Zool.[ogy]. I should like you to try him on that point.

What you say of [Charles] Sumner is very sad. I feel as if he did the best work of any of our statesmen for the country. He certainly would not have stooped to compliment the newly fledged German Emperor by comparing the Prussian Military despotism to our free institutions. — Love to Mrs. P.[eirce] from L. & me.

Ever truly yours
L R Agassiz

Over.

P.S. Shall we not examine the indications of the former presence of the Ocean upon our coasts, as soon as the Spring opens, as I suggested when I last saw you. I feel as if between Pourtalès, Mitchell & Myself we could settle the problem. Even in his new work, only 2 month out, [Charles] Lyell makes the Ocean sweep over Birkshire & the rest of Massachusetts in a comparatively recent period. But I do not believe a word of it. If the three men to whom I propose to submit the matter could spend a week in Pittsfield together they would settle the question.

LA.

Unofficial.

U. S. St. Hassler
Talcahuano, Ap. 20 1872

Dear Sir,

I do not know if Prof. Agassiz
& Capt. Johnson have mentioned in their
letters some differences of opinion which have
arisen between them about some parts
of the voyage; if so, I have thought you
might like to have my view of them.
My opinion never was asked by Prof. Agassiz,
& seldom by Capt. Johnson, which may render
my view the more impartial. With
regard to the abandonment of the visit
to the Falkland Islds, I know nothing at
all. It was not discussed in my presence.
With regard to going into the Rio Negro,
& the Rio Sta Cruz Capt. Johnson asked
my advice, showing me his instructions
and the charts. We both agreed that
the latter were totally insufficient, having
been made nearly forty years ago, during
which time river bars have changed

Louis François de Pourtalès to Benjamin Peirce
On board the *Hassler*
April 20, 1872

UNOFFICIAL.

U.S.St. Hassler
Talachuna, Ap. 20, 1872

Dear Sir,
   I do not know if Prof. Agassiz & Capt. Johnson have
mentioned in their letters some differences of opinion
which have arisen between them about some parts of the
voyage; if so, I have thought you might like to have my
view of them. My opinion never was asked by Prof.
Agassiz, & seldom by Capt. Johnson, which may render
my view the more impartial. With regard to the abandonment of the visit to the Falkland Islands, I know nothing
at all. It was not discussed in my presence. With regard
to going into the Rio Negro, & the Rio Sta Cruz, Capt.
Johnson asked my advice, showing me his instructions
and the charts. We both agreed that the latter were
totally insufficient, having been made nearly forty years
ago, during which time river bars have changed their

position hundreds of times. I considered that the geology of Patagonia, which is known to be exceedingly uniform, had been examined in its principal features in San Matias Bay, and that the other object of Professor Agassiz, viz to collect fresh water fishes, was not sufficiently connected with the plans of the voyage to warrant any risk to the vessel. I therefore advised Capt Johnson against it. In all these cases I believe the Professor acquiesced readily enough. He at least expressed no dissatisfaction [toward me] as far as I know. After we came out of the straits the Prof. was very anxious to pass inside the island of Chiloe, landing at several places to verify some statements of Darwin's. Capt J. agreed to it & anchored at night in San Pedro harbor, inside the southern part of the island. He started the next morning, very early & when I came on deck I found he had turned round and was going to sea again, & Prof & Mrs Agassiz in a state of great indignation. The passage inside of Chiloe is full of islands & rocks & the chart has no soundings except in the bays & along shore. After the Capt. started that morning he found soundings jumping from 15 to 8 & 3 fathoms, not marked on the chart & became uneasy so that he came to the determination not to run any risk, but to go outside & enter at the north end again, which he did as far as San Carlos. I believe the officers all sided with the Captain in that matter. Many vessels take that passage, but not unless they have a particular business there. I think Capt Johnson acted in the spirit of his instructions in not running the risk, though his case was not as strong as with regard to the Patagonian rivers. As Mrs. Agassiz expressed herself rather strongly on the subject, and may have written home in the same spirit (she says the Professor would never have undertaken the voyage had he known how few opportunities for investigation would be afforded him) I have thought you would like to hear all sides.

Very truly, ys
LF de Pourtalès

Cambridge, Oct 22ᵈ, 1872

My darling Ben,

My first letter from Cambridge must be to you. Indeed my happiness in coming home would have been complete, had I found you here. I want to see you so much. Do you know that you left me nearly a year without a sign of life. Now come soon back that we may talk over everything that interest us both most. With the results of this last expedition the Museum is put upon a level with the best. I am sure the materials we have on hand are better adapted to advance science in the direction in which progress is most needed than the collections of any other similar institution, & I would not except the British Museum or the Jardin des Plants from this statement. And yet I have before me difficulties which are appalling, for unless I can take care of all this, the whole may crumble to pieces.

By permission of the Harvard College Library

Louis Agassiz to Benjamin Peirce
Cambridge, Massachusetts
October 22, 1872

Cambridge, Oct. 22^d, 1872

My darling Ben,
    My first letter from Cambridge must be to you. Indeed my happiness in coming home would have been complete, had I found you here. I want to see you so much. Do you know that you left me nearly a year without a sign of life. Now come soon back that we may talk over everything that interests us both most. With the results of this last expedition the Museum is just upon a level with the best. I am sure the materials we have on hand are better adapted to advance science in the direction in which progress is most needed than the collections of any other similar institution, and I would not except the British Museum or the Jardin des Plantes from this statement. And yet I have before me difficulties which are appalling, for unless I can take care of all this, the whole may crumble to pieces. To prevent such a misfortune I must increase the number of my assistants and secure means to buy the necessary apparatus to put up everything that nobody may doubt my statement, or question my estimation of our present position.
    There is one thing in which you may help me. The collections now coming in from the Hassler expedition

were made in the Coast Survey service and you may
perhaps obtain from the Secretary of the Treasury an
order for a sufficient amount of Alcohol to take care of
them, free of duty, which would enable me to go at once
to work with their arrangement. I could pay the price of
the Alcohol, but I have not enough left to pay duty on it;
for it would reduce my means one half. Will you see
Mr. Boutwell, when you are in Washington, and ask
him to grant leave of taking 5000 gallons of Alcohol out
of the bonded warehouses, free of duty, and in install-
ments of a few hundred gallons at the time, as we have
noplace in the Museum to store the whole. In so doing
you would enable me to gain a year in the progress of our
institution & when I am so nearly turning the tables in
our favor in the relative position of scientific collections
in Europe & the U[nited] St.[ates] our Government may
well be asked to do something for us.

   With best love from Lizzie & Myself to Mrs. Peirce &
yourself,

Ever truly your own
L R Agassiz

Our next step must be to prepare such a course of
instruction, that european students, capable of appreci-
ating the difference, may prefer to come to us to finish
their scientific education, than to remain at home. I see
no difficulty in accomplishing this even next year. We
must begin by enticing the master teachers to our

shores, & those who are under a cloud for liberal political views will gladly come & the students will follow & all will be surprised to find what we have already of native vigor & growth.

LA.

My dear friend —

I am so glad you like the article. To me I confess that this fragment, for so it must remain, seems ~~~~~ in a certain sense complete, — it is so manly so simple and clear, so worthy to be Agassiz's last word. Yet I have longed to hear the judgment of his friends feeling that I might be incapable of forming a true estimate of what is so precious to me. I am

By permission of the Harvard College Library

Elizabeth Cary Agassiz to Benjamin Peirce
Cambridge, Massachusetts
December 31, 1873

My dear friend —
I am so glad you like the article. To me I confess that this fragment, for so it must remain, seems in a certain sense complete, — it is so manly so simple and clear, so worthy to be Agassiz's last word. Yet I have longed to hear the judgment of his friends feeling that I might be incapable of framing a true estimate of what is so precious to me. I am perfectly sure that Agassiz believed in no evolution but that which he defines as the normal process of development. The coherence in the geological succession appeared to him purely intellectual existing in the mind which devised and executed all. You will say that this remains true even if the Creator acted through secondary causes and you say that Agassiz would have accepted any true law of evolution —Of course he would — but he had the conviction that the only law of evolution or organic development among animals was the one which has been from the beginning and which we still see going on all about us, — the law of maintenance of kinds by reproduction — I think he believed (but here I tread on ground so sacred that I hardly dare define my thought) that whenever we find the subtle secret for which men seek, it will prove to be very different from any explanation yet offered.

Your suggestion of printing at least a part of Agassiz's directions about the Museum seems to me excellent — They are really very interesting, — would be I think to any one, for they deal more with the large problems of combination & organization than with special details. They would be understood by all and would inspire people with the wish to see the institution carried on for its own sake and not only as a monument to Agassiz.

Ever affectionately yours,
Lizzie C. Agassiz

Dec. 31st/73

COMMENTARY

THE materials of history are fragments of the past which provide us with a partial means of understanding the physiognomy of a body only half undressed. These samples of past events and experiences only reveal aspects of the visible past. But such data must be responsibly interpreted in the spirit of Charles Austin Beard when he termed written history an "act of faith" between the subjective analyst and his public who, despite these constraints, should be better able to untangle the web of yesterday. John Dewey understood this when he declared that historical study requires continual reconstruction and reinterpretation in order to have a significant philosophical meaning for contemporary times—whose quality is also transitory. William James provided historians with a vital corrective to alleged objectivity by affirming that so-called "brute facts" had no meaning at all without the infusion of personal interpretation.

The historian should practice a subtle chemistry upon sources available to him, transforming them, through intuition and personal interpretation, into what Henry James called a vital "sensibility" about the world he reconstructed. This task, undertaken after the actors have left the stage and only the physical setting remains, requires the kind of insight Henry Adams wished he had when he described his lack of knowledge of the "rules, risks and stakes" of the twentieth century game he would be forced to play. Such perception may aid our finer understanding of our transitory present and help in predicting its future. In their attitude toward science, some moderns, sicklied o'er with the pale cast of anti-scientism, may come to appreciate the vision and far-seeing dedication to the life of the mind illustrated by the lives of nineteenth century students of nature. The interdependence of advanced science and culture is vividly exemplified in the ideas and institutions of American society that flowed through and around the life of Louis Agassiz.

The need and significance of such interpretation was characterized by George Santayana who, in *The Life of Reason* (New York: Charles Scribner's Sons, 1953, pp. 421, 426), thus depicted the study of a scientist's life:

Language allows people . . . before their feelings are long past, to describe them in terms which refer directly to mental experience. . . . What a man under special conditions may say he feels or thinks adds a constituent phase to his natural history . . . were these reports exact and extended enough, it would become possible to enumerate the precise sensations and ideas which accompany every state of body and social situation . . . we [thus] actualize appearances . . . but these appearances are true of the reality. That which physics, with its concomitant psychology, might discover in a man is the sum of what is true about him, seeing that a man is a concretion in existence, the fragment of a world, and not a definition.

The documents reprinted in this section, evidence of Agassiz's concretion in existence, provide us with the ability to interpret his life so that the man himself is not a frozen definition. Hopefully, such an effort will provide further insight into those rules, risks, and stakes of the game he played that had deep meaning for him and for our present.

The letters, which deal with ideas and events that had occupied many American scientists since the 1840s, reveal much about the sustenance and intellectual support Agassiz received from his wife Elizabeth, and the power he knew through association with such men as Benjamin Peirce and that group of like-minded makers and shapers of American science who called themselves the "scientific Lazzaroni," and who helped to

establish the Dudley Observatory and the National
Academy of Sciences. The fragments also treat the sciences of oceanography and marine biology, studies of
nature that had fascinated Agassiz since he first ex-
plored American coasts and seas three decades earlier.
Spanning but three years of Agassiz's life, these documents, when associated with other information and
explanation, must be viewed in a larger perspective
than the actual data they report. That viewpoint is,
predominantly, the incredible quest of a man who, at
sixty-three, continued to increase his efforts to domi-
nate American science. Therefore, that viewpoint also
comprises a singular admixture of personal desire and
intellectual involvement, typical of Agassiz's ability
to make congruent a personal project that would, as
he clearly believed in writing Peirce, provide an un-
paralleled opportunity for "promoting the cause of
science generally and Natural History in particular."

The historian must probe into the motivation of
that dynamo-like energy that drove Agassiz ever forward. On the surface, it appears perplexing that this
man, who had such a vast amount of natural history
material at his personal disposal, should seek, like one
dying of an unquenchable thirst, to gain more and
more objects of nature from America and Europe.
Some colleagues wished he would cease both his collecting mania and his engagement in scientific politics
in order that he might gain time for reflection and

concentration on the materials already at hand and perhaps become more tolerant of ideas and men that embraced convictions which differed from his own. But this was not to be. The last three years of Agassiz's life were filled with Herculean efforts to gain $300,000.00 to build an additional wing for the Museum of Comparative Zoology and support more assistants, to establish a predominant role in marine biology and oceanography, and to leave a permanent monument to research and education in the form of the Penikese Island school.

This continual engagement with nature, as Agassiz's first letter to Peirce implied, suggests he took every opportunity to involve himself in large-scale public activity that would make reflection less possible and render less likely the elaboration of such singular achievements as his trailblazing study of fossil fishes, written in the 1840s. Such a manner of coping with the world also reveals that a characteristic attitude of Agassiz's later years was made viable by a synthesis of Lizzie's loyalty, the power of men such as Peirce, and the ever-ripe money tree of Eastern wealth that made grandiose ventures realizable, and intellectual struggles with nature almost impossible. Agassiz seemed to be a man of perpetual motion and aggrandizement, almost as if he feared the solitude that failure to control the scientific establishment would force upon him.

To all outward appearance, the voyage of the U.S.S.

Hassler seemed a typical Agassizian adventure. The entire exploring party contained fifty people. In addition to assistance from the Coast Survey, the venture was supported by a private subscription of $20,000.00, to pay for the instruction of student naturalists and the gathering of specimens. It gained popularity through the presence of interested laymen who ventured forth for education under Agassiz. The ship that left Boston harbor on December 4, 1871, had as its principal naturalists the young zoologist William P. Blake; the German naturalist Franz Steindachner, but recently arrived in America to work with Agassiz; Harvard's ex-President Thomas Hill, pressed into service as an oceanographer; and Count Louis François de Pourtalès, who, with Agassiz, supervised all scientific investigations. Lizzie Agassiz resumed her role of the Brazil expedition, acting as spiritual support to her husband, and as the official public reporter of the journey, through letters written to Boston friends and relatives and articles in the *Atlantic Monthly*—any issue of which, from 1865 onward, seemed incomplete without an account of nature study from her pen.

The principal actors in this last phase of Agassiz's career must be delineated. Pourtalès was an engineer by training, one of that original group of French and Swiss savants who had accompanied Agassiz to the United States in the years 1846–1848. His early interest in marine animals developed into a lifelong career in which he did work of the highest order. Through Agassiz's influence, Pourtalès was aided by support from then Coast Survey Superintendent Alexander Dallas Bache, who granted him permanent posts with the Survey as oceanographer and marine biologist. Since Pourtalès' work formed the basis for teaching and research in marine biology at the Harvard museum, Bache, the acknowledged "Chief" of the scientific Lazzaroni, used government means to advance an Agassiz-inspired research enterprise. Unlike some American colleagues and students, Pourtalès enjoyed excellent intellectual relationships with Agassiz. This was very likely the result of their long association and common European background. But the relationship was always dominated by Agassiz, which possibly explains Pourtalès' unusual criticism at the end of the voyage. By the time the *Hassler* set sail, Pourtalès was acknowledged in Europe and the United States as a marine biologist of first rank. The work of Pourtalès and Agassiz served as both a model and a catalyst for those English naturalists who were striving to gain government support for the pioneering effort in world oceanography of 1872, the voyage of H.M.S. *Challenger*.

Benjamin Peirce and Lizzie Agassiz were people united in their devotion to science and to Agassiz. In 1867, upon the death of Bache, Peirce succeeded him as Coast Survey head and also as the primary link between the scientific establishment and government.

Senator Charles Sumner of Massachusetts was a staunch Lazzaroni politico. After Bache, Peirce, Agassiz, and others of their persuasion had succeeded in establishing the federally chartered National Academy of Sciences in 1863, Sumner joined Agassiz in an abortive effort to form similar government organizations for elite humanists and social scientists. It was natural that Peirce would be gladdened by the news Sumner reported from Cambridge about Agassiz's restored health. Physical collapse had come to Agassiz in the fall of 1869 and lasted for a year, the result of a massive cerebral hemorrhage that had left him partly paralyzed and entirely incapacitated. Even Agassiz's illness revealed the measure of his power. He had been personally responsible for bringing the distinguished French neurologist Charles Edward Brown Séquard to teach at Harvard.

When Agassiz's friend and physician decided he could once again become active, his characterization of Lizzie as "ever devoted and willing to join whatever I decided to do" was a perfect illustration of his relationship with this daughter of Brahmin origins. Elizabeth Cabot Cary Agassiz's career, in personal and scientific communion with Louis, as intellectual and social helpmate to Alexander Agassiz—only twelve years her junior—as a devoted advocate of women's education, and as founder of Radcliffe College, directly contradicts the myth of the stereotypic Victorian lady of manners in a male-dominated society. The careers of Louis and Lizzie were entirely congruent. She was as much at ease as her husband in discourse with the Emperor of Brazil or in association with Penikese schoolteachers. A skillful reporter of science and society, in 1865 she wrote, with Alexander Agassiz, a popular book on marine biology—*Seaside Studies in Natural History* was widely read in schools and in drawing rooms. As co-author with Louis of the highly popular *A Journey in Brazil,* her reports of her husband's involvements with nature were common intellectual fare in proper Boston parlors.

Agassiz's natural history venture on the *Hassler* cruise shared the common lot of all his prior American experiences. Funds and physical assistance came from every quarter. Peirce boasted that the ship, with powerful new engines and iron double-hull construction would have the most modern dredging equipment, to enable Agassiz to realize his plan for establishing American oceanography on a grand scale. The ship would steam down South America's eastern shore, make landfalls where research needs dictated, pass through the Straits of Magellan, and, on its northwestern homeward passage, would visit the Galapagos Islands, the scene of Darwin's notable insights into variation in nature on the cruise of H.M.S. *Beagle.*

On December 2, 1871, Agassiz wrote a widely publicized letter to Peirce describing his scientific expectations for the grand voyage. These were as staggering as every enterprise this large-minded man undertook. He declared that dredging the "deepest abysses of the sea" would yield fundamental knowledge about the origins of the earth and its earliest inhabitants, thereby establishing their significance for theories of organic creation. This belief was a common misconception of evolutionists and anti-evolutionists alike; each believed that the deepest seas would provide knowledge that would yield conclusive data on the origins of life itself. If ancient life resembled modern forms or was distinct from them, this data could support either the evolutionist belief in the derivation of life from a common origin, or the separate creationist conviction of discontinuity in natural history. Nineteenth century oceanographers were never able to substantiate these assumptions.

Typically, Agassiz informed Peirce that he would discover evidence to prove that the great chain of being in nature would show that life was always immutable, as in the present age. He would therefore demonstrate the impossibility of physical causes to explain differences in animals. The permanence that marked all natural history would be illustrated by the fossil forms he confidently expected to find in the great depths of the ocean, types that would be unquestionably similar to those found in the earliest geological periods, thus proving that variation could not have resulted from observable, secondary causation, or physical changes. Finally, the *Hassler* journey would find evidence of glaciation in the southernmost part of the American continent, and provide still another factual barrier to assertions of genetic relationship between animals of the past and present.

By late 1871, Agassiz had begun to feel, privately, the estrangement from intellectual involvement in science that his long association with its institutional aspects had made inevitable. He knew that he had not enjoyed either the time or the peace of mind or body rationally to assess Darwin's theories. Although a prototype of a great adventure in natural history exploration, the *Hassler* cruise was also Agassiz's personal attempt to reassert his intellectual dominance over the science that had been the essence of his life. Like the Penikese idea, it would show the world that Agassiz's personal and intellectual powers were undiminished. At the same time, it would place America in the forefront of oceanographic research, so that Agassiz could perform still another service for the culture of his adopted land.

It was in the spirit of intellectual renaissance that Agassiz was moved to write his German zoologist friend Carl Gegenbauer in July of 1872, having just visited the Galapagos Islands. The letter is a rare fragment of Agassiz's private vision of himself and his relation to natural knowledge. He told Gegenbauer that he had

gone on the journey to improve his physical and mental condition. He had only taken Darwin's books with
him as reading material, because,

> I wanted to study the whole Darwin theory free
> from all external influences and former surround-
> ings. It was on a similar voyage that his present con-
> ceptions awakened in Darwin!

Declaring that he had lived through different fashions
of zoological interpretation in his lifetime, he reflected,

> I no longer leap in with the fiery enthusiasm I would
> have some thirty years ago, but I examine step by
> step, and I must admit that up to now I have not
> made great progress in my conversion to the grow-
> ing doctrine.

In the light of Agassiz's private struggle to see the
world differently, it was unfortunate that the great
promise he and Peirce had seen in the *Hassler* cruise
went unfulfilled. Although the ship undertook the
primary route of the planned voyage, the exploration
was marred and constrained by insufficient planning,
poor leadership, and faulty technology. As Pourtalès
wrote Peirce from Talachuna, Chile, where the ship
had to lay up for three weeks of repair, topographic
and oceanographic information were woefully inade-
quate. Many of the original plans for the journey had
to be given up because of constant failures in the en-

gines and the dredging equipment, leading to that exasperation of Agassiz reported by Pourtalès.

These conditions made Agassiz's original claim that the journey's investigation would disprove evolutionary theory impossible to substantiate technically, even though oceanographers who followed him with superior equipment also failed in this quest. Heralded so triumphantly, the *Hassler* voyage could not be designated as an oceanographic survey. At best, it was a valiant effort to engage in limited land and sea exploration, but the occasional recurrence of illness meant that Agassiz could not function at the height of his powers. In his usual competent manner, Pourtalès made the best of what was discovered in marine biology, publishing some notable papers on the subject, especially good for their analyses of echinoderms. In contrast to the incredible alleged discovery of glacial activity on the Brazil journey, Agassiz did find substantial evidence to support his contention that glaciation had been a significant factor in the natural history of the Andean region.

The dual vision and purpose of Agassiz is significant in view of Pourtalès' affirmation that Lizzie claimed Agassiz would never have undertaken the journey had he been aware of the paucity of research opportunities. Agassiz never made this claim in letters to Peirce or in the published reports of the journey that he and Lizzie wrote independently. Both Agassizes extolled its suc-

cess, ranking it with the Brazil journey in terms of the
wealth of materials collected for the advancement of
American nature study. Agassiz proudly reported to
Peirce regarding two discoveries that flatly contra-
dicted Darwin. In January of 1872, he wrote his
"darling Ben" that a great dredging find proved that
animals of the deepest waters could not be lineal an-
cestors of living creatures as evolutionists had claimed.
Unsupported by evidence, Agassiz lacked sufficient
data to buttress any such conclusion, yet he allowed
it to appear in an official report published by the
Smithsonian Institution. After visiting the Galapagos
Islands, Agassiz informed Peirce that his re-examina-
tion of Darwin's field work demonstrated that the
argument of derivation through descent from a common origin was unfounded, because both the islands
and the nearby mainland were of recent geological
origin. This seeming refutation missed the entire
thrust of Darwin's argument, namely, that the zoological isolation of Galapagos species had inspired varia-
tions from the original type that were preserved as a
result of environmental conditions. The private intent of Agassiz's communication to Gegenbauer thus
yielded to the weight of preconceived ideas.

Privately, Lizzie Agassiz could not mask her dis-
content or her disappointment. Her ennui during
much of the journey was deep; she attempted to re-
lieve it by practicing her German pronunciation with
Dr. Steindachner, and reading *Jane Eyre* aloud to

Captain Johnson's wife. Her thwarted adventuresome spirit led her to complain to her sister-in-law that "the sea is niggard of its treasures . . . I crave a whale or a dolphin . . . and day after day passes and the sea gives us nothing but itself . . ." She wrote Pauline Agassiz Higginson, a few months after the voyage began, that "in the early parts of the voyage I was a little anxious that the many delays . . . for the repair in the ship which we did not discover till we were well underway would interfere with the success of the enterprise and would make your father anxious, too, that he would not have any benefit from it either for himself or science either." Pourtalès' forebodings were partly confirmed, and Lizzie, arrived back in San Francisco, confessed to a close friend that ". . . the voyage so dreaded is over . . . the voyage was so long when we looked forward, and then all the doubts as to the results!"

Agassiz, however, was not capable of public doubt. On returning to the United States, the activist in him took entire command, so that his letter to Peirce of October 22, 1872, placed the voyage in the context of the typical grand venture for which more assistance was needed to ensure permanent success. Indeed, Agassiz could rightfully claim that the specimens gathered by him and his assistants on the Brazil journey and the *Hassler* trip placed the Harvard museum on an equal footing with European institutions, primarily in the realm of marine specimens. This was another reason why the collecting mania could not cease, and Agassiz determined to do all in his power to gain the rich natural history treasures of Europe, and their curators, for the service of America.

The intensification of his collecting efforts also spurred Agassiz's resolve to establish Penikese as a landmark of his conception of research and education in natural history. His privately unproductive *Hassler* experiences made him the more determined to pronounce an ultimate appraisal of the idea of organic evolution, and he planned a series of *Atlantic Monthly* articles for this purpose. He began writing them after his return from the first Penikese summer. It had tired him, and he feared his career was nearing an end. He had written in confidence to a wealthy museum trustee, James B. Schlesinger, stating his intention to make Pourtalès curator of the institution, if Boston's money would provide an endowed professorship to enable his colleague to carry on what he himself had begun. The projected *Atlantic* articles were of great importance to Agassiz, because he still feared that, owing to his failure to keep pace with the intellectual currents of his age, the verdict of history would find him wanting. In 1868, he had written Darwin—after a long silence—declaring his attitude:

I am and have been from the beginning an uncompromising opponent of your views. . . . I hold [them]

. . . mischievous because they lead to a looseness of argumentation. . . . there is nothing in these feelings against yourself, and as to allowing my feelings to be the master of my judgement, I hope I shall never be guilty of such a mistake.

The first, and, as it proved, the last *Atlantic* article —it was published in January of 1874, one month after Agassiz's death—was the reason Lizzie hoped Agassiz's friends would understand his effort. "Evolution and Permanence of Type," however, revealed an Agassiz performing the very mental maneuvers he had abjured in his letter to Darwin. In the article, he announced as fixed truths the assumptions that had underlain the *Hassler* cruise, concepts never demonstrated in actual investigations of nature. Hence, Agassiz affirmed that,

> Endless evidence may be brought from the whole expanse of land and air and water showing that identical physical conditions will do nothing toward the merging of species into one another . . . [thus] primitive types have remained permanent and unchanged—from the earliest geological periods to the present day.

Words such as these confirmed the regret of Agassiz's colleagues in their recognition that the driving activism of his later years prevented dispassionate re-

assessment of evolution. That final appraisal, in what
came to be known as Agassiz's "scientific will and
testament" held:

> Darwin's theory . . . is thus far merely conjectural
> . . . he has not even made the best conjecture pos-
> sible in the present state of our knowledge. The
> more I look at the great complex of the animal
> world . . . the more do I regret that the young and
> ardent spirits of our day give themselves to specula-
> tion rather than to close and accurate investigation.

Agassiz could not help but understand that, of these
spirited young men, many of whom had worked with
him since the early 1860s, most of them, including his
son Alexander, had already accepted the concept of
evolution. It is understandable that Lizzie felt com-
pelled to write Peirce affirming the validity of her
husband's involvement with nature. Agassiz's personal
sense of his role in history is revealed in a letter written to *Atlantic* editor William Dean Howells in November of 1873, when submitting his evolution article
for publication:

> I have already had this MS copied three times and
> I would remodel it again did I not fear to delay you
> by retaining it longer. I send it therefore as it is,
> with the express condition that I shall receive *three*
> proofs as soon as it is set in types . . . I have too much
> at stake in this Article to be willing to allow it to

appear without the severest criticism and keeping it for many days before me in its revised form.

Agassiz could not realize this desire, as his final illness struck a few weeks after writing Howells. Elizabeth Agassiz's effort, then, should be understood as an honest attempt to preserve the essence of a fragment that accurately described her husband's conception of nature. Her letter was a careful statement of ideas Agassiz had expressed many times. She wanted Peirce, and by extension the public, to realize that Agassiz could only believe in "development" as such change was defined by his early training as an embryologist. The concept of process or the multiplicity of change was therefore entirely foreign to his thought—a man who only recognized change in individuals such as the development from embryo to adult, a process that was determined, fixed, and had a final result. She was entirely accurate in affirming that the maintenance of types by reproductive development represented the only kind of "evolution" Agassiz could ever accept, a belief at complete variance with Darwin's view of the world.

If some colleagues saw Agassiz's intellectual end as tragic, Lizzie, who knew him so well, could not fail to understand that the dominance of American science and its institutions was the essence of his American career. She, properly, did not want this vital aspect to be forgotten. Her suggestion that Agassiz's 1863 plan for the organization and management of the Museum of Comparative Zoology remain as a permanent monument to Agassiz's definition of nature study showed her understanding of the passions that drove him ever forward. The regulations had been the result of Agassiz's keen disappointment with the way in which some of his American students and assistants thought and acted as established, independent researchers, capable of full entrance into the domain of scientific activity. True to his European training, Agassiz had given these men orders that the Museum would be organized and run by him and for the benefit of science as he defined it. When they protested his seeming arrogance, Agassiz summarily dismissed them from their positions at the Museum. He then issued formal regulations that, in fact, did much to professionalize American natural history: Students would have to show evidence of original research work to gain museum appointments; no employee of the Museum could work on his personal collections within its walls except for the Museum's benefit, and fledgling naturalists could not "publish or present to learned societies anything concerning their work at the Museum without the previous consent of the Curator." For Lizzie Agassiz to identify these rules as a "monument" to her husband illustrates her insight into how deeply Agassiz identified his activism and authority with the universal promotion of science in America.

The concretion in existence which Lizzie Agassiz felt vital to explain provides the present with a constituent phase of a man's natural history. That history, as seen in these letters, illustrates the operations of a mind in nature that never lacked for a project or an explanation of organic creation, even though the secret of his true physiognomy was only rarely revealed.

ACKNOWLEDGMENTS We should like to express our sincere appreciation for the assistance received in the preparation of this volume from numerous individuals and institutions. Especial thanks are due:

Donald J. Zinn, Department of Zoology, University of Rhode Island

Lillian B. Miller, Historian, National Portrait Gallery, Smithsonian Institution

Norman S. Rice, Director, The Albany Institute of History and Art

William Bond, Librarian, The Houghton Library

Dr. Nathan Reingold, Editor, *The Papers of Joseph Henry*, Smithsonian Institution

The New York Public Library

Marine Biological Laboratory

Woods Hole Oceanographic Institution

The Frick Art Reference Library

Publication of this manuscript was facilitated by a faculty research grant of The Graduate School of the University of Delaware.

This essay represents certain interpretations of national development that will be elaborated in the author's forthcoming volume, *Science and American Democracy* (Oxford University Press).

If the publishers have unwittingly infringed the copyright in any illustration reproduced, they will gladly pay an appropriate fee on being satisfied as to the owner's title.

Library of Congress Cataloging in Publication Data

Lurie, Edward, 1927–
    Nature and the American Mind: Louis Agassiz and the Culture of Science.

    Includes bibliographical references.
    1. Agassiz, Louis, 1807-1873.   2. Natural history—United States—History.
    3. Naturalists—Biography.   I. Title.
QH31.A2L83   500.1.'092'4   [B]   74-933

ISBN 0-88202-011-0